It Could be
WORSE

A girlfriend's guide for runners
who detest running

Beth Probst

CONTRIBUTERS:

Meredith Ziegler, Carrie Okey, Carrie Alajoki, Alisa Kolwitz,

Tami Unseth, Roberta King, Tara Kay, and Courtney Montoya

Dedication:

This book is for every woman who has felt unworthy...

but showed up anyway. You are my inspiration.

Table of Contents

A Runner's Note

This book is about finishing. It is not about winning a race, enhancing your performance or setting a new world record by utilizing some ultra-hip training plan. This is simply a book of tips, tricks and tales about what happens when you want to be a runner and…

In other words, running is not central to your breathing. You are a strong believer that running is a means to an end. That running is exercise. That the running culture is cool and you aren't sure that you have a place within it, but you want to show up anyway. You don't know where to start. More importantly, you don't know if you belong or have earned the right to show up.

I am clinically defined as morbidly obese. My doctor would say I'm active and have great overall health (due in part to running) but that I could stand to lose weight. She's motivating and an amazing primary care doctor, so she doesn't focus on numbers, but all the wisdom on Google says shedding a hundred pounds or so would be good for me.

My background is in marketing. I have absolutely zero authority or knowledge in terms of the advice I'm going to share in this book. So why read it?

Think about it for a minute. Statistically speaking, if 1,000 people line up for a race and there are ten medals, then 99.1% must lose the race in order for ten to win. Yet, every training book on the market focuses on winning races. Sure, the challenge may be about winning the race with yourself – setting personal records, enhancing your performance, and realizing the sacrifice this takes – as opposed to actually winning top competitive honors. Don't get me wrong. I'm super-competitive and I love to win. I also know that in order to win, you have to do the work. And I'd suggest that sometimes a hobby should be based on a self-imposed dare, just for fun.

Where is the book for the individual who is tired of believing they can't run successfully because of some arbitrary standard they've heard over and over again? That somehow their waistline determines if they are worthy, or worse yet, capable of finishing a race. That someone this size, my size, couldn't possibly cross a finish line without seriously hurting themselves.

I'm going to call bullshit on that. In fact, that's exactly what I did, to start. In 2011, I ran my first half marathon. Spoiler alert: I didn't die and I didn't finish first. But I did it. The reality is, you can too. If you do the work, or heck, even if you don't do it all, you've earned the right to line up and prove to yourself that your grit, determination and desire is just as strong as that of the person next to you. Equally important: you can still have a life. You can make a conscious decision to say that running a race is just one part of your being. You can decide, "I want to run, and work full-time, and be a great mom, and enjoy cocktails with my friends and occasionally skip a

Saturday run and eat a pizza." Will that have consequences? Sure. You'll likely land in the back of the pack with me. Frankly, the view is better and less crowded on my end of the course. The cowbells aren't quite as loud. The crowds at the finish line are thinner, as is the line for the post-race port-a-potty visits, and if you are really lucky, you may still score a hot shower. Heck, the medal is even the same.

Over the years, I've read a lot of books, listened to a lot of podcasts and sought the advice of many friends. Some of them even agreed to contribute to this book. Their essays and words of wisdom come from a vantage point much further up the finishing line, but have inspired me to keep going when I was definitely ready to quit. I've attempted to share this wisdom with a little bit of humility in the hope that it will remind you what you've always known; that you are a runner if, and when, you choose to run.

So, if you have ever had a longing in your heart to line up for a race, but allowed that insecure, internal voice tell you that you aren't good enough... this book is for you. You are good enough. You belong. You will crush your goal of running a race, but you will do it on your terms. So buckle up and learn why being last is sometimes best.

Prelude

My first marathon memory dates back to the 90s. I was sitting near the finish line of Grandma's Marathon in Duluth, Minnesota, watching hordes of people push themselves to the brink. It was one of those hot, humid days that make Minnesotans long for winter. To escape the heat, I wandered away from the crowds toward the bay. It was then that I noticed a man hunched over, an aluminum blanket wrapped around his stick-like figure. In his hand, he cradled a massive sub, ready to be devoured. Before eating it, he made a rookie mistake. He placed it on the hood of his car and wandered back toward the trunk.

I cringed, anticipating what would come next. Within seconds, like a scene from Alfred Hitchcock's *The Birds*, seagulls descended on the sub. The man screamed and made a desperate, feeble attempt to scare the birds away, but the damage was done. The man, hunched in a fetal position, looked utterly defeated. These are the moments Nike should showcase in their ads.

Part of me felt for him, but a single word escaped my mouth: "idiot." The sentiment wasn't directed at the man for being a clueless tourist in Seagull Central, but for opting, or more specifically, desiring to do this whole marathon-running business. I walked away in disbelief.

Fast-forward to today and I'm skimming *The Non-Marathon Runner's Guide to Running a Marathon.* Without a doubt, I am losing my mind.

It started with a simple dinner party featuring a menu chock full of cheesy appetizers, hearty burgers and brats, summer sides, fatty desserts and an open bar of margaritas, mojitos, beer and plenty of wine. It was a perfect summer night with amazing weather, meaningful conversation and extraordinary people.

At nine pm, one of the guests announced that he needed to make an early exit. It turned out he was running a 5K at midnight that night, followed by another race at seven am the following morning. As he wandered to his car, the conversation of running came up. One of the more athletic guests at the table mentioned that she was taking a break from half marathons. This, of course, came after she completed the Grandma's Half Marathon at six-and-a-half months pregnant.

While far from athletic, I am competitive, and the conversation (combined with one too many mojitos) left me feeling a bit pathetic. This feeling passed as another round of drinks was poured and I came to the conclusion that they were in fact the crazy ones, not lazy-me.

Something had changed. On Saturday, I rolled out of bed later than usual. A dull ache rang in the back of my head. While glancing at the clock, I acknowledged that I had wasted the better half of a morning on a glorious summer day. As I made my way to the shower, I thought back to the previous night's conversation and to running. As the competitive wheels started spinning in my head, I realized running might be one way to address the lackluster results from my recent annual physical. And, with my impending 35th birthday just a few years away, (wherein, rumor has it, your entire body shuts down), I figured: if not today, when? It was at this moment I decided tot run a half marathon. It was June 30, 2011.

Folklore says that when asked why anyone would want to climb Mount Everest, Sir Edmund Hillary replied, "because it's there." Profound, I know. It was this very sentiment, coupled with a fresh Mojito and a few marginal medical results, that drove me to pick up a book that I had purchased at a garage sale and promptly shelved over a year ago. Glancing at a calendar, I determined that the premiere fall race in northern Wisconsin was a mere fifteen weeks away. The race course was flat, scenic and full of walkers who use the race as a way to enjoy a Fall walk in the woods. It seemed like the perfect fit for the non-runner who just wants to show people she can finish a race. What I didn't know then was that nearly ten years later, I would still be running, the athletic idiot would be me, and I'd still be on a quest to prove that, in fact, anyone can be a runner.

Chapter One

Training

I'm going to let you in on a little secret. While I'm borderline plus-size, I'm active. By active, I mean I enjoy hiking and do make weekly visits to the gym (in pre-COVID-19 days) where I spend time socializing and making modest attempts at getting my heart rate up. It turns out, even this minor degree of regular movement will help prepare me for what's about to be the toughest physical challenge I've set out on.

After flipping through the first few pages of my training book and spending several hours on the internet researching how to avoid losing a toenail while running, I decide it's time to take action. The great thing is, day one of training doesn't really involve running. Instead, it's primarily walking.

I head outside into the bright July sunshine, proud that I'm following through on my goal. I start walking. But then I start to get bored. It seems like if I am going to be a runner, I should be running. Fast. So, I take everything I had spent the morning reading and promptly discard it, in favor of following my (untrained) gut instinct to just run.

I run. It isn't pretty. Within thirty seconds I am panting and my legs are indignantly questioning why I'm ruining what was a lovely walk. Due to improper support, my boobs are bouncing around like jello and with only the sound of my own panting to break the monotony of my feet slapping the pavement, I quickly become unamused, then utterly exhausted. I round the corner, fearful someone might see this humiliating display of athleticism, so I slow to a crawl. I hunch, attempting to fill my lungs with air, and realize one does not wake up one day and run a half marathon.

Once I catch my breath, I resume walking. After all, that's what I'm supposed to be doing, anyway. It's during these moments when I have the first of many, many pivotal moments where I find myself on the verge of quitting. Nobody knew about my plan to run. Nobody would care if I didn't run. Frankly, right now, exhausted after a mere minute of sprinting, I could say one hundred percent, without a doubt, I am not a runner.

I work my way home. My feet hurt. I'm hot and sweaty in the unforgiving afternoon July sun. Mosquitoes taunt me, reminding me that I am, in fact, a loser. Who was I to think I could just start running? By the time I arrive home, I feel defeated.

This isn't the first time I've run, only to find myself out of breath. However, this was the first time I did it intentionally, with the thought that I would run thirteen miles.

Nobody likes to be average at something, especially me. Why would anyone choose to be mediocre? No, thanks. As I enter the house, I plan to put this silly notion to bed and resume my average existence as a non-runner. I flop on the couch and flip open a Diet Coke. Within seconds, the can is half-drained. I grab my laptop to get the latest updates on Facebook, when I notice the browser full of inspirational running quotes still open. I'd been reading them while attempting to get my mojo on, pre-run. One quote immediately jumps out at me. It is entirely cliché, but John Bingham hits home with a simple quote: "The miracle isn't that I finished. The miracle is that I had the courage to start."

Lazy-me says to close the browser and move on with life. But another part of me wonders how much worse it could really get than my maiden "run". All 240 pounds of me had geared up and run, even if only for one minute. I hadn't died. In fact, I probably could have gone much longer if I had followed my training schedule. Lying on the couch, I decide that maybe I should give this another shot. That perhaps I shouldn't listen to my gut, but instead follow an actual training program. I re-read the first few chapters of my guide and decide that tomorrow will be a better day. Tomorrow I will start over, while taking today's lessons to heart.

Day two is much better. Which leads to day three, day four, and... year nine. The crazy thing, though, is even after a dozen-plus races and hundreds of training runs, the hardest part remains lacing up my shoes and just starting. As challenging as mile ten or eleven may be in a half marathon, the mind games I play with myself about getting out and running are incomparable. The excuses are endless. The weather is never quite right and treadmills are hard on my knees. Over the years, my mojo has ebbed and flowed, but for the most part it still tries to get in my way when it's time to lace up.

Another thing that hasn't changed is my love for Googling training plans. I think part of me is seeking that perfect plan that isn't a ton of work but yields awesome results. Let me save you the trouble of doing the same. It doesn't exist. The truth is, training is hard. Even for those of us who just want to finish, you have to put in the work.

Training Tips

Google "beginner running plans" and expect to be inundated. Add to that the number of apps, podcasts, books and other training tools out there right now and you could spend a lot of time researching and not running.

Over the years, I've modified which plan I'm using based on certain milestones in my life. That said, there are a few time-tested plans that have fed my inner desire for minimal days training and maximum results. Don't confuse this with ease. Instead, consider it a "manageable" approach.

Dawn Dais and her 20-week Half marathon Training Schedule: This plan is from my first- and one of my favorite- running books, called, *The Non- Runner's Marathon Guide for Women.* I went from mojitos to the finish line in my first race using this book. This is also the plan I used in my first race after having a baby.

Hal Higdon and his portfolio of training tools. I'd guess some would call him a running god. I've used a variety of sources from him, including his app and his novice running plan. I've perused his half marathon training book and have opted-in on various training plans, depending on my mood. While I don't think the two are directly connected, it was under Hal's plan that I had my best PR and finally cleared the 15-minute per mile mark on a half marathon.

Runner's World. I'll be honest, for years I subscribed to *Runner's World* because I figured that's what runners who love to read did. A few issues in, I actually discovered I loved reading the entire magazine. There was a wealth of information I found useful in it, and it became my go-to source for information and inspiration on a number of occasions. They have a whole suite of training plans that have been helpful over the years. What's even crazier is in 2012 they actually interviewed me about my insecurities around running.

These resources and the individuals who created them are smart. They are trained and educated individuals who base their plans on science. I strongly urge you to find a plan that fits your lifestyle and then use it. But in general, here's the scoop:

Most of these plans are very similar. In general, your longest run before a half marathon is eleven miles. Each week, it's good to get out at least three times and do a pace run, a shorter but fast run, and a long run. I generally saved my long runs for the weekend. I discovered over the years that if your goal is to finish, it's really about consistency. Cutting a six-mile run to five miles won't prevent you from finishing. Starting a plan and getting to week five and then taking a four-week break because you lost your mojo (yes, that's a real thing), that's a different story. If you're a gal like me: you might as well acknowledge that you're starting over at square one at that point.

It's also worth noting that muscle memory is a real thing and adrenaline helps. These two things will help you substantially on race day. But, in order to have muscle memory, you need to build it first. Adrenaline might carry you two to three miles, but it can't run an entire race for you.

Just Start
By Alisa Kolwitz

I love running! It's hard to believe that I was so apprehensive about starting. I didn't feel like I could be a runner. Important things I've learned about running:

• Stretch and then stretch more.
• Warm up.
• Have a training plan if you want to run a race.
• Invest in good shoes, bras, pants and socks.
• Don't eat seafood drowned in butter the night before the race.

If you don't feel like you can be a runner, but you want to try, here are a few of my experiences. Laugh with me and be encouraged. If I can do this, you can too!

Beth, first I just want to say that you are an inspiration! I met Beth shortly after she had her son, and just before I had mine. We became friends on social media, and I would see Beth's posts about her training runs,the races she was planning on and her finishing pictures. I thought, "this woman is so cool. I want to be on her level."

So, I got brave one day and made plans with a friend to do a local 5k color run. It was so scary just signing up. I'm not athletic in the slightest. In fact, I have balance issues and I often trip over my own feet. I'm overweight and basically deaf in one ear. So, you know, a perfect mix for grace and agility. I should also mention that I'm really good at making excuses for myself. My inner voice can be very mean.

But as I got going and started to push myself a little harder and started to praise myself for meeting my goals, I started to really enjoy running.

Lumbering along at a frightfully slow pace, two sports bras on, and my thighs chafing, I did my first color run. Well, I didn't actually run the entire run. I took lots of walking breaks to choke on the colored powder, but it felt so amazing to cross the finish line. It was my mini-Olympic moment. Two very sweet volunteers patted me on the back and handed me a cookie. My husband met me at the finish with our son and it just felt glorious!

I was so pleased with my progress that I just kept running. I would get home from work, feed my family dinner and go on a run every other day. It became my happy habit. As the weather got colder and the sun set earlier, I eventually had say good-bye to my nightly outdoor run. What I didn't realize was the incredible stress reliever running had been. I really started to miss it over the winter and wanted to get back at it. The only answer for me in northern Wisconsin in the dead of winter was a gym membership. I didn't want to go to the gym and exercise amid actual fit people. People who seem to know what they're doing. No, sir. But that was the only option.

After debating with myself for over a month, I walked into the gym and signed up. Victory! Yay me! I went for it! I put on my new shoes, hopped on the treadmill and then... fell off the treadmill ten minutes into my first indoor run. That was a fun one! Mirrors all over the dang place and me falling off the treadmill for everyone to see. Great. . I felt so out of place. But I wanted to stick with it. Running felt so good I couldn't give it up. So, to keep moving along in my progress, I signed up for a 15k in the spring. To be honest, the finishers metal and swag bag was pretty cool, and they said there would be chocolate at the finish line.

My husband and I made it a mini weekend get-away. It was fantastic. I made a few mistakes, though, such as not actually completing my training. I didn't follow any training guidelines and ended up never running farther than six miles, before the race. That wasn't good training. Also, I went out for seafood the night before the race. This was a terrible idea. As were the three cups of coffee prior to the race. I ended up using a port-a-potty every mile of the race. Finishing the race felt like a huge victory, a burning victory... literally. My pants didn't fit right. I had chafing! So much chafing! I developed a theory: if you do not experience at least one awful chafing episode: you haven't pushed yourself hard enough. Or maybe your pants just fit really well and you are a better planner than me.

Fast-forward a year and after having baby number two I felt like it was time to try a half marathon. Why the heck not? If not now, when? I craved that feeling of accomplishment. So, I started training. The thing about lovely new babies is that they do not care that you need to get in your morning run. They just need and want you. It took more effort training for this race. And I was breastfeeding and needed to pump. But for this race, I followed a basic training plan and ate better. The race itself went smoother. No constant port-a-potty action or chafing. God bless the inventor of compression pants! This time my worst fear was shooting milk at an innocent bystander, or even worse, a volunteer. I'm not a fast runner. But under the fear of exploding boobies, I ran my best time. I do still sometimes fall off the treadmill. It happens, so whatever!

So do it! Jump in and start running. Maybe read a few running articles and stay away from seafood. Just start running. It's amazing.

Chapter Two

The Shoes

I'm not a girly-girl. This doesn't preclude me from a serious fascination with shoes. More specifically, I love buying shoes. I don't always wear them, but I often find myself buying shoes that I could see myself wearing someday. The only problem: someday never comes. On the flip-side, I'm super cheap, so while this probably isn't the best therapy, it isn't cost-prohibitive.

Today is different, though. Today I need to buy real shoes. Not just any shoes, but running shoes. I've successfully completed the first three weeks of training. My reward is a pair of shoes that'll help ensure that I never lose a toenail. I opt for our local running store. I'd heard good things about the store, and since it has running in the name, it would appear they know a lot about the subject.

I pull up to the boutique-style store and am immediately intimidated by the slim plastic models showcasing fashionable sports bras and brightly colored running shorts. While totally impractical for my 42D chest, it's fun to dream that someday I'd be sporting the same. I approach the door gingerly, waiting for the rapid pitter-patter of my heart to slow.

Once inside, I'm overwhelmed. A wall of multi-colored shoes of varying types smirk at me, while I do a once-over of the store's contents. I discover there are three employees and only one customer. Ah, the benefits of shopping mid-week, in the early morning. The downside? Their combined weight totals that of my left leg. I breathe again, still trying to calm the pounding of my heart before slowly making my way toward the lone female sales clerk.

I compose myself, suck in my gut, and walk straight up to her. "I need running shoes," I exclaim, anxiously awaiting some sarcastic response like, "for who?" Those mere words would grant me the psychological permission to retire from running. Instead, I'm met with, "great! How long have you been running?" Just like that I'm accepted into the running community.

The next hour proves to be an interesting blend of science, psychology, style and self-loathing. As a larger gal, shoes are something I always enjoy trying on because even on a bad day, my feet seem small. But, before trying on shoes, the clerk leads me to a treadmill. She urges me to run for several minutes while she records my leg movements to find a pair of shoes better fitted for my style. I'm horrified.

I give it my best shot. As we watch the playback, she educates me about my instep. I hear snippets of the conversation but can't help but focus on how stodgy my calves look on camera. I watch my ghost-white legs pound up and down on a treadmill, my eyes drawn to the colorful fitted tank tops and shiny black fitted running tights designed for flat chests and lean, mean running machines. At best, they'd fit a single arm or leg of mine. My head spins. Who am I kidding?

The clerk notices me shifting uncomfortable and suggests that maybe I try on a few pairs of shoes that fit within my instep category. Finally, something I know I can do. I plop down on the bench and begin trying on a seemingly endless parade of shoes scientifically proven to make me run better. I attempt to ignore the color selection, knowing that this is not a fashion statement, but rather an exercise in toe preservation. By pair six, I'm overwhelmed again. They all feel great. I think.

I drill the sales clerk while apologizing for my ignorance. She never once loses her patience. Perhaps she sees "sucker" written on my head. It's clear that I'm not getting out of this shop without swiping some serious plastic. The more compassionate side of me imagines that perhaps she sees herself a decade or two ago, when she woke up and said, "I want to be a runner." While I'm not jealous by nature, I can't help but believe her road to running was easier than mine.

I ultimately go with a pair of Glycerin 9 Brooks running shoes. The leading factor for my choice is comfort, along with an appropriate instep. A close second factor: they have beautiful blue accents.

Next up, I approach the half-wall of socks and begin grabbing various brands, colors and thicknesses. I read each tag carefully seeking any hint that the socks promise to save my toenails and keep blisters to a minimum. Odor-eating, sweat-wicking, plush socks quickly become keepers. Before I know it, I've committed to buying over a half-dozen packages of various types of socks. The final price tag rings in over $200. It's the most I've spent on shoes and socks in a single transaction, ever. The price seems worth it given the fresh injection of confidence it provides. As I finish up my purchase, I learn from the sales clerk that the race I'm completing is actually flat with a slight downhill slope. Up until this moment, I'd never even factored in how slope could impact my training. Regardless, I'm delighted to learn this snippet of useful knowledge, and I view it as an unexpected but welcome bonus from this informative and friendly running store.

Walking away, I'm filled with a new sense of "yes I can!" For the first time, I can't wait to get home, lace up my shoes and hit the trail. My thoughts flow easily as I whiz down the highway at 65 miles per hour, with a simple press of the pedal. Why can't running always be this fun?

Tips for Choosing The Right Shoe

Here's the thing. There are a lot of shoes out there and a lot of opinions on which shoe is best. I'm not going to add to that. Here's what I will say: as uncomfortable as it is, go to a running specialty store and ask for help. In particular, find one that'll analyze your gait and help determine what type of arch you have so that you can narrow the 10,000 options to at least a single shoe category. I understand this may feel awkward, but the momentary discomfort is much more brief than that of dropping $150 on a pair of shoes, only to have aching hips and knees on day one of your training.

If you don't have access to an expert, there are some at-home ways to "map" your arch. This is a good starting point. I'm not sure it's 100% reliable, but the gist is that you dip your foot in water, then stand on a napkin and see where your arch contacts the napkin. When I tried this to bypass going to a store, I just made a big blob. That said, my arch is neutral so that makes some sense. A simple Google search will provide you with video tutorials and directions to navigate the anatomy of your arch, but I honestly cannot over-stress the value of going to a real running store.

Once you've determined what category your foot falls into, try on lots of shoes and see what feels right. Do not rush this process and buy the first pair you try on. Also, DO NOT think about what looks cute on your foot and certainly don't ask about the color options. In other words: think function, not fashion. Next, please don't try to squeeze yourself into a size seven when you are really an eight. The reality is that you'll probably need an eight and a half or nine in this scenario. If the sales person pushes on your big toe and says you need a size up, TAKE THEIR ADVICE. I can assure you, the embarrassment of buying a larger shoe size is nothing compared to losing a toenail during sandal season. While this might happen anyway, a tight shoe almost guarantees it.

Once you have a pair you like, see what the return policy is for your shoe. I'm a huge fan of Brooks. For whatever reason, the Glycerin is made for me. I've now owned over twenty pairs. That said, when I thought I'd be cool and do a trail run, for whatever reason, Brooks' trail running shoes didn't work for me. They had a great 30-day return policy which I unfortunately had to take advantage of. I ultimately landed on a pair of Saucony shoes. I needed a wide toe box for the elevation change on trails. How's that for sounding tech-y? But seriously, Brooks' generosity for accepting a return that just didn't work made me a loyal customer for life on a line that ordinarily works for me. Some specialty stores have a similar policy, so be sure to ask.

One you have a brand and style you like, be prepared to endure annual shoe changes. The only thing shoemakers love more than rolling out new lines is updating their current lines. I've been known to buy a pair or two on eBay when they've updated the model and have ended up an unhappy camper. I've also purchased extra models during their close-out season. *Runner's World* does a "best shoe" guide every spring and fall. This seems to coincide with when new models drop. Spring seems to be the best time to land a sale on last year's model, at least for the brands I purchase.

Lastly, women's running shoes, in general, are bright. Embrace it. Sure, you can find neutral colors. But if there were ever a time to wear outlandish, obnoxious, neon shoes, this is the time. While fifty shades of blue tend to comprise the color palette I lean toward, I've been known to sport some hot pink and purple shoes as well, along with plenty of yellow and green. If not now, when?

Any Body Can be a Runner
By Carrie Alajoki

Everybody can have a "runner's body". If you are on the fence about becoming a runner, you are literally the only person standing in your way. Don't wait until you've lost weight, until you feel more comfortable in your body, until you look how you think a runner should look, or until you reach that perfect size in your head. Seriously, just start now. Don't wait. There will never be the perfect time in your life when you aren't busy juggling personal and professional obligations.

I did not start running until I was in my 30's. I have struggled my whole adult life with hypothyroidism and polycystic ovarian syndrome and the dreaded weight gain and depression that goes along with both of those. I have worked through complicated and devastating ob/gyn and pregnancy issues. One of the most difficult aspects of medically related conditions is the inability to control what is happening to your body. Even when you take excellent care of yourself through diet, exercise, emotional, intellectual and spiritual care – there are just some things you can't control.

I am the type of person who likes a good challenge. If you tell me I can't do something, I will try to prove you wrong. I really don't do well with being told no. Not allowing obstacles to prevent you from completing something you set your mind to can be a positive trait that will help you reach your goals. On the contrary, always trying to prove you can do something someone thinks you can't do is exhausting and not productive. It took me a long time to admit I don't do well with being told no. It also took me a long time to realize there are things in life some people just can't do no matter how hard they try, how hard they wish for it, or how bad they really want it. For example, I will never be an Olympic athlete, I will never play on an elite competitive team, and I will probably never be a supermodel. Those things are just not going to happen. They won't happen no matter how hard

I work or how hard I pray, and they won't happen if I read personal development books that say, "if you put your mind to it, you can do anything." Folks, I am sorry to say, there are just some things I can't do. That statement took me years to be ok with.

Running is not one of those things. Running is not something you can be told you can't do. YOU are the only person who can tell you running is not for you. Sure, the running world can be intimidating and overwhelming at first. Running in public where people can see you is scary. What will they think? Running on the treadmill in the gym for the first time is terrifying. Will people laugh? Showing up to the start line at your first race is frightening. Will I finish? OMG will I finish last? The negative self-talk and worry can be endless. I don't look like the other runners, I am not trained enough for this, I don't belong. Running can also seem complicated. What shoes do I wear? What gear do I need? What app do I use? How do I fuel for a run? How do I foam roll? The list of considerations for "how to be a runner" seems endless, overwhelming and daunting.

My advice to someone who has always wanted to try running but is apprehensive in taking that leap is to first give yourself permission to say, "I want to be a runner." The next step is to just get started. Really, just start. Don't worry about the right gear at first, buy a pair of comfortable shoes and get outside. Once you are outside, start small. You have to be ok not running a half marathon on day one. Walk a block, jog a block, repeat. Keep doing that until one block turns into two blocks. It does not matter the pace or the distance. Just move and keep moving. I remember the first time I ran a full mile without walking. I remember the street, time of day, and the feeling of success.

After you have completed your first day of running – yes, literally your first day – switch your mindset from "I want to be a runner," to "I am a runner." There is no secret mathematical equation that calculates the pace and distance that qualifies you as a runner. You do not have to finish your first 5K or run a full marathon to call yourself a runner. You are an accomplished runner on day one. Dig deep, be brave, and don't let anyone tell you that you are not a runner. You are the only person who can say that. Running is not easy. Some days are better than others. Running is a rewarding physical challenge that will push you to overcome your fears. While there might be some things in your life you will have to be ok with not accomplishing. Running is not on that list. Do not take no for an answer.

Chapter Three

Food

My legs aren't cooperating today. Last night in a moment of celebration I ate an entire highrise Jack's pepperoni pizza. Sure, I shared my crusts with my reliable bestie Joey (the dog), but otherwise, I downed the entire pizza. I woke up sluggish but confident that I had officially carbo-loaded for today's six-mile run.

By now, I'm pretty used to six-mile runs. I'm still slow but I don't start with the overwhelming doubt that I won't finish. Today I'm having doubts. Once on the road, I'm confident my blood will start pumping and this sluggishness will be replaced by heart-pumping goodness. After mile one, I find that isn't in the cards for me.

It's about this time that my stomach starts to move. At first, I feel things sloshing side to side. As I push myself up a rolling hill, my innards seem to be pushing upwards too, begging to find release. I pause, catching my breath, welcoming the notion of ridding myself of these extra carbs. Despite my noble efforts, nothing happens. I have no choice but to continue running. By mile two my stomach settles as a heavyset ball, bound in my gut, happy to have ceased jostling around. At mile three, I turn around, confident that I'm going to finish. But then, gravity takes over. What was jostling around and begging to go up must now go down and out.

The large lump in my stomach presses down harder, begging for release. My head starts racing. With three miles left to go, the only "release point" is over two and a half miles away. "Ugh!" I exclaim to myself, knowing that holding this ball in my gut will be nearly impossible. And, of course, I'm running in a residential area where I have no place to hide.

I run faster, quickly discovering that such movements are not good for keeping things settled. I slow down, knowing that the longer this run takes, the less likely it'll be that I'll outpace an embarrassing conclusion.

The next forty minutes are an exhausting, humiliating combination of short spurts of running followed by doubling over and showcasing my best turtle waddle, begging the gods to let me make it to the privacy of my home. I don't make it.

The warm sensation runs down my leg. This instant relief is immediately followed by absolute defeat. My bright blue running shoes are now spattered with a muddy substance that reeks of bad eating habits. Why would anyone in the world do this to themselves?

As I approach the house, my husband is relaxing on the deck. He jumps up, "how'd the run go?"

"I don't want to talk about it!" I exclaim, stomping past him toward the bathroom, holding back tears of humiliation. I stand in the bathroom looking at the mess surrounding me, knowing that my husband is on the other side of the door. I cannot face him.

I hop in the shower, fully clothed and start rinsing my pants, shoes and socks as the tears flow freely. Over and over I ask myself, "why do I do this to myself? I'm not a runner. I am a plus-size girl who thinks eating an entire pizza is normal. Real runners don't do this. I'll never be one. Ever. I'm done."

Once I'm convinced that all the evidence has been washed down the drain with my salty tears, I'm faced with yet another conundrum. I'm stuck in the bathroom with a single towel and a pile of shit-stained clothing. Between me and my room, and dry clothes, my husband stands at attention waiting to understand what's caused this recent outbreak of crazy.

I slowly crack open the door and peer into the hall. I see him at his computer. I cannot sneak past. "I'm done running," I say, holding back more unexpected tears.

"What happened?" Two simple words. I realize the y only option that will allow him to truly understand how done I am with this horrific sport is to be brutally honest. "I pooped my pants! That's what happened."

Silence. My husband's head spins as he calculates which words of support and wisdom he can shed on this moment, knowing it counts.

"Shit happens," he says with a grin.

All of my humiliation and running rage is immediately redirected at this man. I literally hate him. "This isn't funny! Your wife just pooped her pants by our neighbor's house. What if someone saw me? Do you have any idea how horrified I am?! I'm never, ever, ever running again. I'm done." I say with all the pride a towel-clad, tear-stained, defeated woman can muster.

"No you aren't. So, you had a bad day. Tomorrow will be better. But you'll keep running," my husband says.

He's right. I know he's right. And he knows that I know he's right. This is just one of the many ways over the years that he'll show up for me in my running journey, providing me the fuel and encouragement I need to keep going. But right now, I hate him. The thing is, tomorrow is a new day. As much as I hate to say it, the next day is better. As is the day after.

Nothing worth doing in life comes easy. The same rings true with running. I didn't become a runner when I dropped $150 on a pair of real running shoes. Nor did I become a runner when I woke up one day and said, "I'm going to train for a half marathon." Truth be told, I'd still call myself a runner if I hadn't finished that race.

I certainly didn't become a runner, in my mind, when I hit rock bottom, squishing my way home and praying that someone would end my misery. I became a runner when I hosed myself up, laced my shoes up and returned to the road telling myself, "you can and will do better." I became a runner, when shit happened, and I showed up anyway.

Eating Tips

I have absolutely NO credentials or expertise in nutrition. I do have the motivation of never wanting to crap my pants again. Over the past ten years, I have read every running and diet article I could get my hands on, with a focus on reducing indigestion, avoiding muscle cramps and dehydration, and having enough energy to not pass out. Beyond that, I live in a world of moderation where nothing is off-limits. I eat meat. I eat sugar. I buy non-organic fruit and vegetables if the organic ones are cost-prohibitive. I enjoy full-fat potato chips. But twenty-four-hours prior to a long run (which for me is 6+ miles) and then during and after the run, I do try to follow these basic rules. For me, it really works:

Day before:
- Drink lots of water. I aim for 100 or so ounces.
- At least one of my water bottles includes a packet Nuun. I swear by the stuff. If it's early in the morning, I'll do a Sport+ (after 3 pm, it'll be non-caffeinated.)
- Avoid high fiber foods at all costs. This includes salads and, most importantly, baby carrots. Baby carrots do bad things to my stomach during a run.
- Munch on pretzels, or if I'm craving something sweet, a moderate-sized Rice Krispie bar.

Night before:
My focus is to eat a heavy, simple carb dinner with a small portion of protein. My go-to meals include:
- White spaghetti noodles with a homemade meat sauce.

- Swedish pancakes (made with white flour) topped with syrup and scrambled eggs on the side.
- Grilled chicken sandwich on a white bun and lots of pretzels. At this point, I avoid things like mayo, cheese, bacon or anything else that makes a chicken sandwich incredible.

Before Run:
- Nuun Sports+
- Black coffee with a splash of almond milk
- ½ bagel with creamy peanut butter
- Banana
- Plain water

During run:
- Water at least every two miles
- Jelly beans (I stock up at Easter. Starburst ones are particularly delicious and much more cost-effective than the sport beans you can buy at a running store).
- Ibuprofen

After run:
- Banana
- Water
- Large latte or Coke
- Ibuprofen
- Simple recovery protein/carb combo. Think: peanut butter toast.

Race Day:
- Same as long run, but I do treat myself to a coke two to three hours before the run.
- If due to traveling, my breakfast is more than three to four hours before start time,I may eat a Nature Valley peanut butter granola bar about an hour before I run.
- Water at all of the stations.
- In a half marathon, I'll allow myself a shot of Gatorade at one or two stations, if needed. I really try to avoid energy drinks while running and instead eat cheap jelly beans. I'm pretty confident no other running book will support this recomendation.

After the Race:

- Same as my after run plan. I also enjoy a whatever-I'm-craving celebratory treat meal. This often equates to potato chips and Top the Tater. This chip dip is the food of the gods that has a small regional reach in distribution. Unfortunate for you, but wonderful for me. If I'm craving something salty, I go that route or I have a massive ice cream cone if I'm craving something sweet. This is generally post-half marathon. For 10k races, I tend to focus on a fun celebratory restaurant meal.

Real Eating Tips

For runners who want to try a diet that may actually help with performance, try *Run Fast. Cook Fast. Eat Slow*. This book is co-authored by Shalene Flanagan and Elyse Kopecky and is a sequel to the running website and cookbook called *Run Fast. Eat Slow*. My love for this book derives from its simple recipes that look fabulous. And these gals, who are real professionals, focus on healthy outcomes and whole foods versus calorie counting and macros. For those of us just trying to feel good, that's all we need. Obviously, I could stand to listen to more of their advice, and if I ever transition to eating the right foods, this will be the first source I rely on.

Fun Fact

I buy one to two bags of jelly beans every Easter. My favorite is the Starburst brand. They last me a year. I usually have a baggie of 20-30 in my pocket on all long runs. I find these are one-tenth the cost of performance jelly beans, taste way better and provide the same shot of glucose I need to fight off fatigue. I avoid GU at all costs. It is also important to note that if you carry a bag of jelly beans with one or two Ibuprofen in it, be sure to look at what you throw in your mouth. There's nothing worse than thinking you're about to bite into a soft, sweet jelly bean, only to discover it is ibuprofen… and you're a solid mile from a water station!

Chapter Four

The Necessities

After six-weeks of training, I'm starting to discover that while new shoes and socks are great, I'm still not loving this running thing. Sure, my feet feel better, but other things are out of whack. I decide to schedule a luncheon with a gal who happens to work for Grandma's Marathon.

While we're enjoying a hearty helping of Mexican food, she mentions she's noticed my Facebook postings about starting to run and inquires if I'm thinking about doing a 5k. Armed with the new-found confidence a pair of Brooks shoes brings, I boldly tell her I'm not just starting to run but I'm actually doing a half marathon in a few months. She looks at me like I've lost my mind. Perhaps it's because I'm saying this while munching on an endless bowl of chips and salsa. The truth is, she's seen what half marathons do to people like me. I think she feels pity on me. A true friend, though, she quickly hides her disbelief and offers immediate support. She even fills me in on some great tips about protein shakes. Within minutes we're talking about training schedules, sports massages, carbs versus protein and the race course. By the time lunch comes, it almost feels natural to have categorized myself as a runner.

The problem with proving yourself to someone else, in your mind, is that at some point you have to take action and follow through. The next day, I head back out on the open road. I've reached the point in training where I'm transitioning from tracking time to actual mileage. I'm also realizing just how slow I am. As good as the Brooks shoes are, it's still my legs that need to go the distance. By mile three I'm breathless and I still have another mile to go. I'm 33% into my training but I can't even run 33% of the race. A single thought invades my mind, "I'm screwed." Now, what? All I know is I have ten weeks to figure it out.

My training book gives me two days off per week. This sounds like a lot. It is not. I have just started a new job and my freelance side job is booming. Add in the craziness of summer and the fact that my runs take a long time and I am starting to stress out. I need more hours in my days. I know, who doesn't? I also need more energy. I needed to find it fast. Meanwhile, I've plunged head-first into training for a race, and have no clue what I was really signing up for. I've never run on the course or looked at the map, and other than what I had learned from the store clerk about it being a downhill race, I know nothing else about it. The super-planner in me resurfaces. I may not be able to run 13.1 miles right now, but I can at least plan for my anticipated inability to run. This thought, paired with a chilled glass of wine, my lounge chair on the deck, and a wireless connection, leads me to do some homework on what I'll actually be in for.

I log on to the Whistlestop Marathon website. It's here where I learn that this year's event is the fourteenth annual race. Unlike a road race, this course runs along an old railroad bed that is now a popular snowmobile and ATV trail. Rumor has it that the packed dirt course is easier one one's knees than asphalt. The race takes place during the peak of fall colors in northern Wisconsin. As someone who was married on marathon weekend, I'm well aware that temperatures around that time can range from thirty degrees and windy (like my wedding day) to an 85-degree Indian Summer day (like my second anniversary).

I print out the maps. The clerk at Duluth Running Company wasn't lying. The race course ranges from a slight decline to utter flatness the whole way. I look up race results. My stomach sinks. I was currently clocking eighteen-to nineteen-minute miles. It appears this speed would put me close to last place. It also shows that racers running the full marathon will more than likely pass me or potentially run me off the course. How humiliating.

I mention these new-found facts to my husband. His empathy is overwhelming. "Who cares," he exclaims. "This isn't about winning. It isn't like you're competing. I'm just really proud you're doing it."

My blood pressure spikes. Why not just stab me with a dull spoon and pour lemon juice in the open wound?! Don't get me wrong. My husband is extremely supportive—especially in terms of this latest insane idea of mine. He's promised to pay my entrance fee, chauffeur me around, and offer positive reinforcement along the way. He also lives on planet Earth and realizes that up until six weeks ago, I did not run. At all. He recognizes that I'm pushing my limits (pretty much to the max) just planning on running a half marathon with a mere few months of training. To him, this is more than enough. But, to someone who aims for greatness and is extremely competitive, this is mediocre at best.

I start to obsess over the previous year's finishing times. The age breakdown is even more disheartening. In addition to finishing near last, I will certainly be finishing last in my age category. No one with any degree of pride sets out on a race anticipating they will finish last. In fact, I rarely do anything unless I think I can win. Or, at least place close enough to the front that I can find a reasonably sane excuse for why I didn't finish first. I have a hunch this is an ongoing issue I'll struggle with up until race day.

I try explaining my reticence to my husband. He attempts to reason with me. "You realize that lots of people aren't even racing. Or, they are racing the 5k because they don't have it in them to do the half, right?" I don't buy it. At this point, I'm not buying anything he's saying. I've pitched my tent in the land of self-loathing. And I have weeks to go.

I once thought I didn't enjoy running. I now know it without a doubt. Runner friends keep talking about this rhythm I'm going to find one day on the trail. It appears to be MIA for me, because after weeks of running, it still sucks. I've tried running to upbeat music, county, hip hop, podcasts and even Christmas music. Nothing helps. Instead, I find myself slogging along patiently waiting for the moment when my run is over. It never seems to come soon enough.

Don't get me wrong – I'd be lying if I said I wasn't seeing changes in my running. In fact, I now consider a mile run a warm-up. In the past, this would have been my entire run. The one downside, though, is the longer I run, the slower my average mile turns out to be. In other words, seniors walk faster than I can run.

This is disturbing on several levels – in part because I love to walk, and I'm good at it. Truth be told, I could walk 13.1 miles tomorrow and actually enjoy it, especially because this course is entirely flat. And, I could probably walk it faster than I'm running right now. But I've made up my mind to run. Anyone who knows a stubborn Finlander will tell you that this is non-negotiable. So... the suffering continues.

To add insult to injury, I'm not losing weight. I never started running to lose weight. In fact, that was one thing I said I wasn't going to stress over during these three months. I figure one form of torture is enough. But you know how sometimes you say you're not expecting something, but deep down you sort of assume that something will happen? Yeah, that's me with the digital scale right now.

To pile on the fire even more, , while driving home I have the misfortune of hearing a conversation on Wisconsin Public Radio centered around being average, with author Dave Martin who recently wrote a book entitled *Dare to be Average*.

The show gets me thinking about what being average means and why it sparks such a negative reaction. By definition, average is - well - average. It should be expected. It is in many regards, the norm. But if that's really the case, why does it seem so bad? To make matters worse, I won't even be average in this race. I will be below average. In fact WAY BELOW average. Mediocre. Last place. The literal definition of a total loser.

Growing up, I was taught that everyone is a winner. That I could be anything I want to be. The sky's the limit. I should dream big. Well guess what? Everyone isn't a winner. In fact, there's generally only one winner. And while I can strive to be great, I cannot, in reality, be anything I want to be. I don't want to be below average, mediocre, or worse yet, not complete the WhistleStop Half Marathon. But the fact is, these are likely my only options.

Nobody strives to be an under-performer. No one excels by finishing at the bottom rung. And as much as I want to tell myself that by being at the bottom, I'm allowing someone else to be at the top, it doesn't help. I'm not that charitable.

My pity party is only mitigated in some small measure by the fact that I'm noticing my rear has become a little more rump-like. It's a small but discernible change that only one who glances analytically at one's own rear would notice. Do not think Kim Kardashian-rump. Instead, think of something a step down: from a large, square butt to a-little-less-than-large oval butt. This, my friend, is progress. It doesn't ease the sore calves or self-loathing that comes with knowing I'm a loser. But if it's the only consolation prize available, I'll gladly take it.

It's during this time that I realize I need to double down and get serious. Shoes were a great investment and helped motivate me to this point in my training. My toenails are all intact. But that isn't going to carry me to the finish line. I had recently started experiencing backaches, and a lackluster sports bra meant plenty of upper-body bouncing. Now that summer humidity was in full swing, the cotton t-shirts that had seemed so cute were no longer serving a function beyond creating chafing and hot, sweaty spots. And my so-called "running shorts"? At best, they were designed for someone who enjoys the sensation of walking with a cozy semi-snuggy. I figure the energy I exert trying to constantly dislodge them exceeds the calories burned by actual running.

I've reached that pivotal moment in training when I need to challenge myself to make some real admissions. To acknowledge that if I'm going to be a runner, I need to start thinking like one. Real runners recognize that there are some basic investments that matter. Things like sports bras, sweat-wicking clothing and compression gear. If you're plus-size, you know athletic wear is beyond intimidating. The truth is, especially in 2011, you can get cute plus-size leisurewear that may look sports-like but is not sports-appropriate. Or, you can drop a small fortune in the hope of finding some off-brand company that recognizes that people over 200 pounds can, in fact, run, and need technical support and reinforcement much more than our 32A counterparts. I'm not judging. Let's be real – I'm a bit jealous. But maximum-support running bras serve a 42D-gal much more critically than a waifish 32A-lady . I'm just sayin'. After much research and feverish scrounging, I find several wins online from companies that I respect. Over the years, I sometimes even see these items in a store. Those opportunities are rare, but appreciated.

Accessory Tips

The best advice I can give on this front is to set a budget early on and then plan to double it. No – seriously. I always thought running involved shoes and sweats. As a kid, that's true. As an adult, especially as one who's motivated by shiny new things and wants to ensure I don't find myself chafed and sans toenails? Well, the investment is there.

Bottoms:
I prefer running pants if there's a shot I'll run into someone I know. That said, I've determined that compression shorts or capris are the bomb. A lot of times, I wear them under black yoga-type pants if temps allow. What I do know is that in order to find the right bottoms, you need to act a bit foolish in the dressing room before hitting the roads. Trust me, it'll save you a lot of hardship in the end.

A word of advice - cheap tights don't stay up. I have taken full advantage of online sales, only to discover that cheap running tights fall down and often you don't even notice until it's too late. Once you do, you're basically forced to waddle-walk while holding up your pants with one hand. As a result, I do a series of burpees anytime I'm trying on new bottoms. If after five of them the tights are starting to slide, I immediately discard them. If they survive that test, I jump up and down and run short sprints in my changing room to see how they wear. If they budge an inch, they don't stand a chance of staying on me.

Then the sticker shock comes in. On what planet should you spend $80 on a pair of running pants? The planet where you don't want to show your skivvies to a crowd of strangers at the finish line. My go-to brands, in part because they can be found in an XL and XXL, include Brooks and Under Armour. Most recently I added a pair of New Balance, because of the slick cell phone pocket that's built in.

Why these brands? I got hooked on Brooks after I fell in love with their shoes. Under Armour is something I took a liking to because I'm a huge fan of Lindsey Vonn. I know she's paid to wear their clothes, but, come on! Lindsey skied a race with a broken back and is one of the most inspirational athletes I've ever seen. If she can train wearing Under Armour compression-ware, then it can only help me, right?

Shirts:
My shirt preferences are similar. Both Brooks and Under Armour have great lines for people my size. Under normal fashion conditions, I find myself attracted to statement shirts. I love funny tank tops, Sisu-inspired quotes and shirts that make me feel like a badass. When temperatures spike, I'm looking for the loosest and coolest clothing I can stand to wear without looking like a complete fool. You will never find me in just a sports bra but you may find me in a sports bra and tank that is so oversized that you question the validity of my fashion. That's okay.

Sports Bras:
Speaking of sports bras, you're going to really want to take your time on this one. I'm a 42 - 44DD. First off, finding sports bras sized that large is not an easy feat. When you do, they're often low-impact versus high-impact. Don't buy a low-impact bra if you are a plus-size running gal. I repeat: DO NOT buy a low-impact bra if you are a plus-size running gal! I don't care how cute the bra is… you will pay dearly for that decision. I should know. I did it more than once. Bottom line: if you're an ample-busted gal, you will want something that's going to compress those bad boys as much as humanly possible. After many rounds of bras, I've come to love three brands: Glamorise, Brooks and SheFit. They all offer a mid-to high-impact underwire sports bra that can withstand the wear and tear of me not "remembering" to air dry and gentle wash, while also providing much needed support during a pavement-pounding run. I tend to wear the Brooks Moving Comfort MAI on jogs and trail runs, whereas my Glamorise Underwire High Impact model withstands longer and faster pavement runs. The Shefit Ultimate Sports bra is my latest investment and leaves me feeling a bit like a badass.

Headgear:
Then there's headgear. This is hard to get right. You want headwear that'll breathe, for when you sweat, but keep you warm if the wind picks up. I live in northern Wisconsin so it isn't unusual for me to be running in twenty degrees one day and sixty-five degrees the next. I've run races when there's a sleet/ rain/ snow mix, but I've ended up sunburned at the end. After nearly a decade of seasonal running, I now own a stack of headgear that covers most conditions. In the summer and on warm/humid/wet days, go with a simple ball cap with a mesh bash that breathes. Right now, I'm sporting a Made for More hat from Rachel Hollis and a hat that showcases the greatest of the great lakes – Lake Superior. In spring and fall, I tend to ditch the ball cap for a handknit stocking cap that has a lot of holes in it. The goal of this is to insulate my head but allow for plenty of ventilation. The one I wear

most frequently was a three dollar clearance score at Old Navy that I purchased on a whim. On days that dip below thirty-five degrees, you'll find me sporting merino wool caps or winter hats with a wick-away feature built in. My go-to brands include Merrell and Under Armour.

Underneath my caps, you'll almost always find me with earbuds. The quest for the perfect earbuds has plagued me for years. For the first few years I used ten dollar Sony wired earbuds. This way I wouldn't feel bad if I lost them and could replace them as-needed. I'm sorry, but ear and head sweat is a real thing, and well… I just didn't want to deal with cleaning them. After a while, my husband decided to treat me to a pair of BOSE wireless earbuds. They were awesome. Right up until I put them in the washer. Plus, I was always stressing about losing them. This is why I can't have nice things. Between worrying about misplacing them, forgetting them somewhere, or breaking the wire that goes behind your head, it was just too much. Anyway, after that, I started buying cheap wireless earbuds. Here's the thing – if you go that route, you'll be frustrated. I can't count the number of times I'd be thirty minutes into a run and with no warning the ear buds would die. Batteries were a constant problem and the quality was either great, or if my phone was in my pocket or the wind was blowing, the crackling would drive me crazy. So, I did what every connected 42-year-old runner does: I turned to Facebook. A runner friend hooked me up with a pair of $30 wireless earbuds called Sbode. I love these. The quality is great but the cost is such that if and when I wash them, I'll still feel they were worth the investment.

Tracker:
Shirt, bottoms, bra, hat, earbuds. Seems reasonably adequate, right? Think again. The last major investment I made involved a running tracker. Because honestly, if it isn't documented somewhere, did it even happen? And yes, those memes of runners who go back and forth in front of their driveway to get that last 1/10 of a mile to hit their goal for the day – that's totally me. This was a tough decision that's evolved over the years.

When you count your runs by steps, not miles, it's critical to know exactly how far you've traveled to ensure you don't over-train. Keep in mind my goal to do the bare minimum. At first, I attempted to drive my running course and use my car odometer to gauge my mileage. I quickly abandoned that notion after determining many of my miles would involve shortcuts through the woods, back-country trails and lakeshore jogs. I needed something accurate.

After much debate, I invested in FitBit. For years, this GPS-enabled watch served me well. When it finally broke, I discovered (in my haste to purchase a new FitBit) that my new model didn't have a built-in GPS. This is a non-negotiable feature for me. Today on my wrist, you'll find a beautiful Garmin 235. This watch does everything I need and more. In many ways it's my emotion-free accountability coach that gives me real-time feedback on how to improve. It was certainly an investment but after three years of owning it, I'm confident it was worth every cent.

The bottom line is that no matter what your needs may be, there's likely a running accessory to fulfill it. Some of them are more necessary than others. Some will literally transform your running experience. And many will just give you that added boost of confidence and motivation to keep moving.

Just Keep Running
by Courtney Montoya

"We should run the Delano (Minnesota) Fourth of July 5K together. I will train for it and then we can run it together," my brother Nick said. Little did I know that we would never get our chance to run together. My brother passed away a year later on September 9, 2001, when he was 19, when I was 22.

When I was younger, I was pretty active, running around with other neighborhood kids and playing games, so I was an average-size girl with a good activity level.

During high school I participated in a lot of academic activities but wasn't into sports which led to a more sedentary lifestyle. I was the one who avoided having to do the timed one-mile fitness run, or just walked it instead of trying to run it. Toward my later years of high school, I weighed between 220-240 pounds and was not in good shape, so running was something I avoided at all costs.

When Nick and I had that conversation, I was home from college. Most students gain weight in college, but thanks to a great fitness center close to my dorm, I had actually lost weight and gotten in better shape in college. This is what had prompted our conversation.

After college I did maintain my weight loss by eating healthier and consistently going to the gym or taking fitness classes.

Fast forward to 2010 and my friend Sara was interested in running a 5K. I wanted to do it to honor my brother and to know I could do it. We chose the 5K at the Minnesota Landscape Arboretum. We thought spring would be a nice time of year weather-wise and it would provide beautiful scenery, which it did. However, neither of us realized the amount of hills that would be part of the course! We both survived and got the bug to do more.

I have always had a hesitation to run or sign up for races as I don't exactly have the "runner's build." I've always teetered on being average-to plus- size and am definitely not breaking any speed records. It's easy to think those thoughts like, "I'm too big to run," or "Everyone else makes it looks so easy," but through the years I've realized that everyone runs for different reasons: health, personal challenge, the enjoyment of the outdoors, or just to have some quiet time to think.

Everyone is thinking about their own race and everyone supports one another and cheers each other on. Whether you run a six-minute mile or a fourteen-minute mile, it's the same finish line and the same mileage. There were a couple things that helped me when I started running:

- Start small. There are several programs available online like Couch to 5K, which will start you out with a running/walking combination. If you try to do too much too fast, your body probably won't react well. Also, make sure not to increase your distance too fast.
- Reach out to runners in your circle. It's always nice to have advice from current runners or be able to get opinions on things along the way.
- Don't worry too much about speed when you first start. Getting the mileage accomplished was my first task. Speed will come with time or by using specific speed workouts.
- There will be good days and bad days and sometimes there is no reason why. Throughout the years, I have tried to analyze the "why" but I could never establish any consistencies. Be happy with the good days and move on through the bad days.

I have run several 5Ks, 10Ks and two half marathons since the first 5K, through ridiculous heat, rain, and sometimes through snow and ice.

The half marathons were definitely races where I had to dig deep to reach my goal to finish. There is nothing like crossing that finish line after thirteen miles and knowing that you did it. For someone like me who used to try to get out of running the mile in the gym, it was pretty unbelievable to think that I achieved that.

I'm not sure I will ever complete a full marathon. The time commitment for training for a full marathon is daunting, and I'm just not sure I love running enough to do it, But I never say never.

Chapter Five

Race Week Jitters

Don't do it… As I type the words, I already know I'm going to regret the results. But just in case you're wondering, as I was at that moment, yes - you can die from running a hal marathon. A quick Google search results in 72 million hits about super-healthy folks dropping dead from the exertion of running. Okay, so maybe they weren't all healthy but MANY of them were in the best shape of their life. Welcome to race week jitters.

The race day countdown is at three. My running plan strongly discourages any last-minute attempts at getting just one more training run in. I've discarded any last-minute hopes of ditching a few more pounds or somehow improving my time by a few more minutes. The momentum from my eleven-mile run is a distant memory. Instead, I'm full of fear.

Running logic says that if you can run eleven miles one weekend, then the next step in one's training is 13.1 miles. There is absolutely no reason that I cannot or will not cross that finish line. Except logic has taken a backseat to fear. Instead, all I can picture is getting to mile eleven, only to have my body give out on me. I literally visualize myself seeing the eleven-mile marker and then collapsing from exhaustion.

In addition to the fear of dying, there is also the fear of failing. Maybe I'll run too fast in the beginning, only to find my tank empty at mile twelve. What if I trip on the transition from gravel to pavement? Or I discover that Powerade is not my thing and my stomach can't tolerate it. What if I get leg cramps? Or my heart stops? Or I can't make it to one of the porta-potties dotted along the course? I'm not sure where this fear is coming from but it is front and center.

Let's recap for a moment. Fifteen weeks prior, I was not a runner. Now, without a single race under my belt, I'm going to run through the fall forests of Bayfield and Ashland counties on an old railroad bed for a piece of metal. I've completely lost my mind.

These nagging thoughts consume me over the next 48 hours. I'm a competitive person by nature and a planner by trade so these what-if scenarios are not entirely unfamiliar thoughts to me. I like to know what I'm up against and do my best to prepare for the worst.

But, here's the thing: I'm acutely aware that I don't know what I don't know. I turn to my finisher friends online and ask the question, "How did you know you wouldn't die your first race?"

More than one responded, "I didn't." If nothing else, at least my friends are honest. You couple this with the number of like-minded crazies out there, and it's easy to understand how I ended up in this predicament. But, the I didn't and You're crazy were also followed by what I needed more than anything… encouragement.

Fitness guru Fred Devito once said, "if it doesn't challenge you, it won't change you." It is one of the many running memes you will see if you ever search online for encouragement. It's also a sentiment many of my friends echoed, testifying that one of the greatest senses of accomplishments they ever experienced was crossing that finish line for the first time.

That to push yourself past the seven-mile wall requires you to dig deep and achieve something you weren't a hundred percent sure you could finish. It was in those moments, that they discovered they were capable of so much more than they ever dreamed of. They experienced the empowerment that accompanies that discovery.

My training transformation moved me from "you're crazy" to "you're an inspiration." Let me repeat that for the folks skimming, in the back. Me. The fat girl. An inspiration to a friend who could likely outrun and outpace me in a heartbeat. They see me as an inspiration. Regardless of what happens next, I am different. Still, I allow myself to dwell on the fear. I verify my emergency contact information. I remind my husband that if he gets a call from an unknown number during the race, he better answer specially if it's from a 715-area code.

The race calendar ticks down to one day. Today is the day I pick up my packet. Today is the day I aim to win a carbo-loading competition. Today is the day I shift from "I can't" and "what if I can?" to "I will" and hopefully, "I did!". I allow myself to believe that all of the mosquito bites, sweat-drenched, early Saturday morning runs weren't for nothing. They had a purpose – and that purpose was to prepare me for this moment.

I'm a hard-core Finlander. My blond hair does not come from a bottle and my big bones (but not the padding) are a product of my ancestors. I am made to thrive in tough, brutal conditions. What many folks don't know, though, is there's something else that comes with being a Fin. Sisu.

There is no adequate English translation for this sentiment. It's an inner strength, drawn from will, determination, perseverance, and the ability to act rationally in the face of adversity. Sisu is not momentary courage, but the ability to sustain that courage. That's the closest approximation to a translation that I can make. For me, the best synonym that comes to mind is "grit".

Today, my Sisu is alive and well. I've prepared for this moment. I'm afraid. Sure,

I lack confidence. I fear the unknown. But I dig deeper. I remind myself that I don't quit and I will be fine. If I honestly believed I was going to die, would I line up for this race? Absolutely not. Truth be told, if I make it to mile eleven it will take an act of God - or a very strong security team - to drag me off that course before I get my medal.

I carbo-load. Oatmeal and a banana for breakfast. Rice krispie bars and pretzels as snacks. Grilled chicken sandwich for lunch, and more pretzels. So many pretzels. I finish work a bit early so that I can head over the expo and pick up my race packet. Things are getting very real.

I walk into the Brettings Civic Center and my heart drops. I've entered a world of twig-like people looking sleek in their compression pants and sporting fancy running shoes. Everywhere I look I see lean muscle-machines. At least it feels that way. I wade through the sea of spandex and line up in the half marathon line. A woman casually asks me, "are you in line for 5k pick-up?" "No!" I exclaim. My head starts reeling. Am I that out of place? Why would she think that? Who am I kidding? "Do you know where the line is? This is my first race and I'm a bit lost." Oh. So maybe her question wasn't about me but instead just another fellow runner trying to wade her way through the chaos that comes with packet pick-up. I point out the sign for the 5k and wish her well. I suddenly find myself at the front of my line. It's time.

"Name?"

"P-R-O-B-S-T."

"Elizabeth?"

"Yes."

"33-years old?"

"Yes."

"Here you go. Enjoy the race!"

I wander outside and look down at the manila envelope in my hand. Inside are the keys to the kingdom. The badge of honor I'll pin to my Under Armour shirt to grant me access to run this race. The tag that'll inform race course volunteers what finisher shirt I get when I cross the finish line. The badge that'll capture my first personal record. I feel the tears welling up inside of me. Anxiety, fear, doubt, but more than anything, an overwhelming sense of wonder that I made it this far.

I drive home. My husband is prepping French bread to accompany our spaghetti dinner. The friend who was partially responsible for inspiring my journey is also running Whistlestop. He and a buddy come over for dinner, as well. Together we carbo-load and talk tangents. Let me rephrase that. They talk tangents. The last time I talked tangents was high school geometry. I'm perplexed. At first I think he's kidding. But, as he draws out the last quarter-mile of the race and the number of ninety-degree turns in it, I realize he's serious. He's concerned about the impact it'll have on his time and the strategy he's entertaining to ensure the shortest distance. My two guests ultimately place in the top five in their division. But right now, he's actually worried. My friend, the runner who has completed dozens of races, is nervous?!

Our fears are drastically different. His concerns can be measured in seconds and might be considered a bit more strategy-based than fear-based. I, on the other hand, am now realizing that the two of us are lining up in the same spot. I recognize that if I line up incorrectly, I may get run over by these folks who are banking their wins in seconds, not hours.

"So, how do you know where to line up?"

"Fast folks up front. Slow folks in back. In the middle, you just ask around for people's finish times. Find your people and you'll be good."

Sounds simple, right? Don't kid yourself. A future me will make the rookie mistake of lining up in the back of a race in Door County, Wisconsin. The race starts on a narrow trail within a state park. It was probably five minutes to start time and I was in the zone. My earbuds were in and the only direction I was looking was forward. I thought most folks were lined up. It turns out that many of the folks who were hanging out when I lined up weren't spectators, as I thought. They were bundled-up runners. In that five minutes, they shed their clothes and lined up behind me, (unbeknownst to me). When the gun went off, I started casually walking and I could feel this force behind me. I turned my head and all I could see was a sea of runners. I could feel their energy pressing urgently at my back. A polite runner would have stepped out of the way. I was afraid and the tree-lined course and line of spectators left me nowhere to move aside. I ran as fast as I could. It wasn't fast enough. I felt the humiliation burn as folks weaved their way around me. Somehow, I survived.

I digress, though. We finish our dinner. Wish each other well. Just one more sleep until race day.

I pull out all of my race packet goodies. I verify I have enough safety pins. I double-and triple-check my race outfit. I set three alarms. I drink more water. I stretch. I go to the bathroom a lot. The combination of race day jitters and gallons of water in my bladder results in no sleep. The alarms are pointless. As the clock hits midnight, it's race day. I've made it.

Tips for Addressing Fear

Fear is such an odd beast to tame. Early on in my running journey, my fears were legit. I honestly didn't know what my body was capable of and I was charting unknown territory. As time went on, I realized it was more about my fear of the unknown. My fears were really about my insecurities. The truth is, occasionally a very healthy runner goes into cardiac arrest on the course. Equally true: many runners like me cross the finish line.

I'm not an expert at managing fear. In fact, some might say I utilize my inner Sisu and bad judgment. That said, the best running book I have read that tackles the challenge posed by that little voice with a megaphone screaming, "you don't belong!" is Kara Goucher's book *Strong: A Runner's Guide to boosting confidence and becoming the best version of you.*

I've been a long-time fan of Goucher. Prior to running, I once worked in television news in Duluth, and grew up about thirty miles from there. Goucher hails from Duluth, so her name was commonly thrown around in our newsroom. I loved watching her stories and learning more about her running journey. We're the same age, so we sort of grew up together even though she has no clue that I exist. I, on the other hand, admired her running long before I had any desire to log a mile. Every time we did a story on her, I thought, "wow!" She seemed to be that perfect human who could achieve anything. While I don't resemble those kinds of folks, I strive to be like them.

But back to fear. Goucher calls her book a *confidence journal.* I call it a game-changer. I don't use those words lightly. If you've ever wondered if you belong, then this book is for you. This book didn't exist early on in my running. I wish it had.

The book helped set my intentions and gave me tactical tools to talk myself off the self-doubt ledge in multiple aspects of my life. I attribute my personal record, the reason I didn't quit my MBA program, and a slew of other things to Goucher's book. In other words, read the book, face your fears, and be ready to change your life.

A Word of Advice from Dad
by Meredith Johnson

If I'm being honest, I don't even remember when I started running. Running was always a part of our family traditions. My brother, dad and I would run 5k races while my mother cheered us on from the sidelines. Even though my brother loathed running, he would no doubt leave me in the dust at every race. Primarily, my father was the avid runner who sparked my running pursuit.

It's easy to quit, knowing you won't get first place. Did I ever win first place? Not even close. I told myself that quitting wasn't an option. In track and field, I often took last place in relays, which I normally didn't run unless they needed someone, but I was consistently slow at running. Sprinting around a donut-shaped track didn't make my heart pump (although neither did tossing a cold metal ball, aka: shot put or throwing discus), but I never gave up.

You will have good days, you will have bad days. That's normal. I have those days – and sometimes those weeks – when running isn't in the cards. That's ok. Give yourself the flexibility to run when your soul needs to. If you doubt yourself, remember these words from my father: "There's no such thing as not good enough to run. Running is about challenging yourself. You run against yourself and not against others. Whether it's a mile or ten miles, victory is in doing it and getting that endorphin high. It's the sense of satisfaction when the tasks are completed."

No matter your running journey, learn to offer yourself grace. You don't have to go from zero to sixty in a matter of days. Start gradually to avoid injury. Find a pace you enjoy and settle in. My dad always said, "find your pace and stay there." This was a man who ran ten marathons when he hit 40 and always inspired me to run. In fact, I will always feel closer to family, especially my father, when I run.

We are connected through running, even if he's faster than I am at the age of 60. I will always hear my father's voice while running a 5k with me, "You see that hill? Run fast and run hard!" He was referring to me passing people on the hill. I, quite frankly, was more interested in viewing the veranda while jogging (mind you, it was cow pastures and cornfields, which often brought me peace.) I may not share the same competitive streak as members of my family.

I run for a variety of reasons, not only the family connection. I run to gain some clarity when life gets hectic, or to jam out to ridiculous 90s music. Sometimes I run being pulled by my 25-pound cockapoo, who goes from no-to-go speed within seconds (sometimes I envy her.) Despite many changes throughout my life, running has been a constant. Whether I was trying to fit into a bridesmaid's dress in college or simply meeting new friends in a new town, I have always had running. I've never been the fastest, but I run to socialize, to center myself and to enjoy what nature has to offer. If I'm lucky, I run with my father and his running buddies of 30 years who talk smack and swap stories during their daily five-mile run, something I aspire to.

Running isn't a perfect prescription. It means something different for everyone. Let running be what you need – whether it's time to reflect or to challenge your body to go a little further than previously. Find your intention and "run with it." As dad says, "Set a goal. When you reach it, you set another one and so on."

Don't be afraid to find running buddies who will not only hold you accountable to run, but may end up providing some of your strongest relationships. Some of my best friendships started out as casual three-mile runs, peppered with vents about disappointing dates, filled with curse words, laughter and excessive honesty. The best conversations stem from early morning runs (unedited and pre-coffee) or after work stress-reliever jogs (sometimes with mixed curse words and a cold beverage afterward).

No matter what, never give up. I'm five months pregnant right now and am slow as a freight train, but I don't stop running. Some days my feet are the size of a baseball field, some days I could run five miles easily. It's all about balance. Not every run will be perfect, but it will be yours. Never let anyone ever tell you that you can't run. Be careful comparing yourself to others. Remember this if your journey; no one else owns that. The key is to remember your intention, laugh about the failures and know that there's always room for improvement. And remember, there's also always room in the closet for more running shoes!

Chapter Six

Race Day

The clock strikes five am. I roll out of bed. Turns out I didn't need three alarms. Between bathroom runs and this unfounded fear of oversleeping, the most I slept was two hours.

I check my outfit again. Turns out nothing changed since I checked it six hours before. I can't help but think that I haven't worn my running shoes since Tuesday. This is the longest I've gone without wearing them since that infamous shoe store purchase. It feels odd.

I begin a one-sided conversation with them. "Shoes, we need to talk. I spent a lot of money on you. I can't guarantee that my legs won't fail me, so I'm counting on you. That's why I paid what I did for you. Just please, let me finish. And if you're feeling really generous – with all of my toenails intact and my feet blister-free."

The shoes don't answer. They sit silent and composed. I imagine this is a good thing, from a psychological standpoint. However, I want a sign. I won't get into my religious beliefs in this book other than to say that I like getting signs... preferably positive signs. This morning there will be no signs.

I finish getting ready and head downstairs. My husband is casually munching on a bagel, ready to be my chauffeur, personal coach, motivator, photographer, best friend and spouse. I feel blessed. I proceed to down a glass of orange juice, coffee, water and coke. I begin to feel a little bloated and am grateful that my race pants stretch. I peek my head out the patio door to discover it's about ten degrees warmer than I thought it'd be. This all seems good. Before I know it, we are loading up the car and heading to the start.

This race has a parking lot – or more specifically, an open field – allowing spectators and racers to drive to the start. I will come to learn in future races that this normally isn't the case. Today, I'm grateful I can avoid the bus and instead make my husband stay by my side until I cross the starting line.

We park the car and I assess the situation. Hundreds of men and women are doing odd stretches and running around. I can't help but question those running in circles. Don't they realize they're about to run a half marathon? I, on the other hand, stay inside our warm car until there's about ten minutes to go. For years, for better or worse, I always used the first two to three miles of running as my way of stretching and warming up. I can see the start line in the distance and figure I still have at least five more minutes of sitting in my warm car when my husband suggests (aka forces me) to at least start to wander in that direction.

I hop out of my Forester. My gut hurts. I wonder if I'm going to puke. I realize the pressure is a result of the massive volumes of liquid I drank, and I'm experiencing an abrupt need to relieve it. With just five minutes until race time and a long line at the port-a-potties, I need to make a call that I'll regret for three miles. I decide to hold it.

I line up in the back of the pack. With my tribe. My people. The woman in front of me is wearing the cutest shirt proudly proclaiming she's from Wawa, Canada. "She's come a long way to suffer," I think to myself.

We pause for the Star Spangled Banner. My heart is pounding. I'm overwhelmed with emotion. I reflect on the last fifteen weeks. I'm actually here. I look around and soak it all in. Regardless of what happens, I'm here.

I hear a countdown in the distance. Heads start bobbing. My husband snaps some photos from the sidelines. The countdown hits GO. There's just one problem: we're not moving. It turns out that starting in the back means a pretty slow, anti-climatic start.

The herd starts pushing forward. I feel my legs moving. I tell them to conserve their energy since my time hasn't even started, yet. It takes me two minutes to get to the start. Within ten minutes the crowd has thinned. I find myself with a gaggle of walkers, many of whom are moving faster than me. My body wants to move faster. But, I have thirteen miles to go. I know that passing these people now, only to get trounced in a few miles when I'm a collapsed and defeated pile of flab on the trail, isn't the right thing to do. It goes against every urge in my competitive body, but somehow my logic wins out. Instead, I crank up the volume to the most random playlist I've compiled and attempt to find my rhythm.

Runners talk a lot about rhythm. For me, this means setting a pace that'll allow me to be upright at the end of the race. I soon discovered that one advantage of being in the back of the pack is you soon have plenty of room to run. By mile three, I find myself pretty much abandoned on the course. It's about then that I hit my first water station.

I've never attempted to drink water while moving. And, given I'm not moving very fast anyway, I opt to stop. I down a glass of water while chatting with the friendly volunteer. I get to the bottom of the glass and realize I'm not sure what to do. It seems wrong to throw it on the ground but even odder to hand it back to her. I start to walk away and recognize there is no garbage can. I wander over to the edge of the trail and gently set my glass down. This is a practice I continue through the rest of the race. It's often met with odd stares, but I just can't bring myself to randomly litter on such a pristine trail. I note there's no line at the nearby port-a-potty. I finally relieved myself. I resume running.

By this time, my adrenaline has subsided, and rather than racing, I feel as if I'm out for a Saturday morning stroll. Any thoughts I had about finding some massive surge of energy and cutting my goal time of four hours in-half have dissipated. Instead, I'm focused on putting one foot in front of the other.

Over the course of the next two hours, I find myself thoroughly enjoying wandering through the woods. I cross several rivers lined with colored leaves barely clinging to their branches but clearly wanting to showcase the final remnants of fall. I meet the occasional spectator offering words of encouragement from the comfort of their lawn chair. I admit – I'm a bit jealous of their vantage point.

About halfway through, I finally look at my watch. It's then that I realize that my rhythm has been faster than I anticipated. That, in fact, I might finish thirty minutes sooner than I told my husband to watch for me. This feels good. For a split second, I feel like a winner.

This new-found nugget of optimism gets me thinking. This morning, thousands of people lined up with a common goal: to finish a race. At the end of the day, after all, it's just that. But we each came with our own agenda. Some came to win, to set a personal record, in memory of someone, in honor of someone, to overcome something, to prove something, or in rare instances – because they just love running. Despite our different reasons for running, we'll all get to the finish line by putting one foot in front of the other.

For me, today is about a blend of things. Whatever I do today will certainly be my personal record. Throughout my months of training runs, I've thought about a lot of people, dealt with self-doubt, held pity parties, enjoyed moments of pride, and in some instances, I even had fun. I'm carrying all of that with me today. But what I didn't expect was to feel this sense of accomplishment… this sense of being a winner even though I will without a doubt lose the race itself.

As I come closer to the end of today's journey, I'm met by countless strangers who assure me that I can finish. They ring bells, give me high-fives, hand me water and juice, and share words of encouragement when I need them most. Soon, I start to pause my iPhone during these pockets of empowerment so I can soak in this unexpected kindness without distraction.

I enter Ashland. To my left, I see Hugo's Pizza in the distance. Images of Chicago-style stuffed pizza flash through my head. I'm craving a Diet Coke. And a massive burger with waffle fries. And the Top the Tater I've purchased to eat on my car ride home. Instead, I pop the final ibuprofen I've stashed in the hidden pocket of my running pants. It's the only preemptive action I can think to take, since I know my legs aren't going to love me in a few hours.

In race terms, I'm on the home stretch. In reality, a few months ago, I couldn't run a mile without collapsing. Now, I have a couple miles to go and it again seems insurmountable. A biker comes cruising at me, wide open. I'm not sure if she is the pacer who will soon ride in front of the elite full-marathoners or just a woman on a mission to bike on the race course despite there being thousands of runners on the trail. Regardless, I'm reminded that I could very soon be run over by the full marathoners. I suddenly feel the need to pick up my pace.

I glance at the sky in hopes of a Hollywood moment. How wonderful it'd be if I was suddenly met by some higher-sourced power that would give me the strength to finish. Instead, I nearly trip over a crack in the trail as the 20-mile-an-hour wind cuts at my face. My legs shoot me an urgent message that they're growing weary of this race. I feel the energy draining from them and realize I am running out of gas. I guess this is my moment of truth.

The wall is a real thing. For those who push themselves to the brink, the wall may come earlier. For me, I had conserved my energy for so long that it didn't hit until about mile eleven. The infamous mile eleven. The spot where I wondered, "what happens next?"

The answer: I keep moving. This is something I need to, and only can, finish for me. I pick up my pace. In seconds, I burn past the speed-walkers I had been following for hours. Somehow in this frenzy of activity I've put my iPhone on repeat. "Somewhere Over the Rainbow" is blaring in my ears. I attempt to change songs while running and am met with "She Ain't Your Ordinary Girl." By the third time I hear this song, I can't take it anymore. I rip off my headphones and stuff them in the pocket of my bright blue running coat. Everything suddenly seems deafeningly quiet.

I pass a dozen or so people and endless road crossings over the next half-mile and enter the final 2/10 of a mile. I run wide open. It's the first time I've run this fast since the 50-yard dash in high school. I round the final corner to the dinging of more cowbells and a small crowd of people who appear to be colored specks. I keep running only to notice I'm about to pass two walkers right before the finish line. Momentum gives me no choice since I'm pretty sure if I stop running at this point, I definitely won't start up again. I hear my name over the loudspeaker and the words, "strong finisher." I can finally stop.

I receive my finisher medal. I hear my husband yell my name. I look up in time to see him crossing under the racer only barrier tape to hug me before snapping some more photos. He's never looked so good in my life. We head to the tent to get my finisher t-shirt. I pop a donut hole while my husband snaps even more photos. Random strangers tell me "great job!" And in a single moment, I get why people do this. It suddenly makes sense.

Race Day Tips

This list is in no way exhaustive of everything you need to contemplate race day morning but it's a good start:

- Will I oversleep? (You won't. You'll be too busy peeing.)
- Am I hydrated? (see above)
- Do I have my bib?
- Do I have safety pins?
- Did I eat enough?
- Is my playlist long enough?
- Stretch more?
- Stretch less?
- Is my phone charged?
- Do I need a hat or a visor?
- Sunscreen?
- Do I need extra clothes at the start?
- Where do I park?
- What's the weather?
- Where's the bus?
- Am I on the right bus?
- Where's the starting gate?
- Where's the port-a-potty?
- Are my shoes tied?
- Are my shoes tied too tight?
- Did I eat too much?
- Where's the first port-a-potty on the course?
- Where's my water?
- Do I need to hydrate more?
- Did I eat enough?

I think you get the point. The best thing you can do is channel Bob Marley and hum in your head, *don't worry... about a thing. 'Cause every little thing.... is going to be alright.* Just keep telling yourself that. Over and over again. You've made it. Savor it.

The only useful tips I can give is to time your port-a-potty visits. If you go too early, you'll end up standing in line at least twice (I average two to three stops during shorter races and missed the start of Grandma's Half Marathon for this reason.) If you wait too long, you'll miss your window, especially if lining up toward the front is a thing for you. It isn't for me, so I don't have that issue, but I've seen plenty of runners get frustrated when attempting to jockey for position.

My other suggestion: don't use the sixty minutes before the race to change up your strategy or your pre-running stretches. Everyone has their own way of warming up. Take notes. But don't start emulating the runner who's doing deep lunges as their warm-up if you've never even stretched prior to a run. Not that I did that or anything...

Last but not least, take a selfie BEFORE the race. Take several of them. You look a lot prettier in this moment. You've earned this bragging-right moment. Plus, it's easier to smile. Be as silly as you want. Be as quiet as you'd like. Talk to yourself. Gab with a friend. Wander aimlessly. Do whatever you need to do to show up at that starting line comfortable. I promise you, absolutely nobody is watching you. In other words, just do you.

Chapter Seven

Now what?

I did it. I crossed the finish line. Just a few months after an evening spent drinking a few too many cocktails, I ran a half marathon. That's 13.1 miles, folks. I did it. But now what?

Google running memes and the jokes about running races are endless. I've mentioned the head games I played with myself. And in my quest to be perfect (whatever that means), I'm struggling to savor this moment. As fun as it is to post a sweaty selfie of my fat ass holding a half marathon medal, I can't help but wonder *what if...*

What if may kill me someday. Maybe sooner than later. I find myself thinking about the number that has now become my personal record, or PR, for those who want to sound hip. Obviously, I set a PR because it was my first and only race to date. I immediately start picking it apart. I think of the moments wasted on the course. Was that bathroom break really needed? Or, that selfie on the bridge? Did I really need to stop and drink my water? Or, now that I know I won't die after mile eleven, could I have run faster on miles 1-11? I mean, fifteen seconds faster per mile would equate to 4 minutes off my time. Percentage points in how close my name appears to the bottom of the list.

For those who are rolling your eyes right now, I understand. Up until crossing that finish line, I didn't realize how competitive I was with myself in this running thing. I'm one hundred percent confident I will never cross the finish line first. I'm equally as confident that if I tried again, I could finish faster. As a stubborn Finlander, that means something. It means that the challenge is on to find another race so I can beat myself.

I know that the more you do something, the better you get. I also know how quickly one can erase the gains of training. My ibuprofen hasn't even worn off from today's milestone and I'm already picturing in my head what crossing that next finish line looks like.

A word of advice: if your goal is to do another race, seize this moment. Because friends, it will not last. That Saturday afternoon I savored the congratulatory Facebook posts. I dream of going on a diet and losing the weight and finishing faster. The idea of clearing a three-hour half marathon seems attainable, from the comfort of my couch. After celebrating my victory and savoring the world's longest shower, I plopped on the couch to dream and plan what's next.

I immediately went online to find the perfect next race. It's mid-October and race season is winding down. I want to give myself time to train hard and drop fifteen pounds. I looked ahead to spring. I want a small race. A similar experience. An opportunity to maybe bookend the trip with a vacation. That's when I discovered the Door County Half Marathon. It sounds perfect. A spring run in a closed state park at a tourism mecca, but during a cooler season. Late enough in May that I could focus my long runs in April/May before mosquito season in northern Wisconsin. And the most important detail: race registration was open!

I'm a frugal gal who hates to waste money. I'm also very goal-driven. So, without hesitation, I entered the race. In hindsight, it's the only reason I kept running. As the day turned to evening, the ibuprofen wore off and the runner's high diminished with the onset of sore muscles. By nightfall, the self-doubt boogie man had reared its ugly head again.

Different moments of my big race day replayed in my mind. The self-doubt that creeps in, standing in a sea of lycra and knowing that it wasn't designed for someone like you. The knowledge that in order to lose weight, you would have to actually eat less. The awareness that in order to run faster, you must train harder. It can be a source of disappointment or shame to acknowledge that the best and worst thing about running is that your effort in equals your effort out. When the rubber hits the road (literally), it's just you, your head games and the empty path. These doubts would follow me, and weigh on me, for years.

The runner's high from the moment I crossed the finish line was gone. While I had registered for a race that was seven months out, my running calendar was suddenly clear. The next morning I awoke to no running goal. It was an odd feeling to go from early morning runs three to five days per week to nothing.

Don't get me wrong. I could have just laced up my shoes and went out for a run. Lots of folks do. In fact, I'm friends with several of these folks who don't need a race registration to run. They actually run because they love it. Don't mistake those folks for me. I'm one of those gals who likes running in order to justify the pizza at the end of the day, dropping triple-digits on athleisure-wear, and party-dropping that I just ran a half marathon. It also provides the perfect excuse to skip functions I don't want to attend, due to an early morning run I have to do the next day.

I'm not sure what camp you fall into. If you're still reading my book, I imagine that perhaps you resonate a bit more on the side of running-as-a-means-to-an-end. If so, I HIGHLY recommend that if you want to keep running, sign up for another race. Take some sort of action that'll get you back out on the road. Or maybe you just retire from running. Because here's the rest of this story…

When you go from couch to half marathon in three months, a race seven months away might as well be a lifetime. I had every intention of getting out for a run after taking a week off. But a week turned into two, which turned into four. Then the holidays came. And soon, a couple of weeks became a couple of months. Enter New Year's resolution-time. Time to start training. But it was January. In Northern Wisconsin. You know, the time of year when it's light out for about ten seconds daily and high temperatures are regularly measured in degrees below zero. Motivation is at a premium during this time. The thought of lacing up and running on some icy street – yeah, not so appealing. Before I knew it, it was February.

I rallied. I ran. But I was starting all over again. There was no muscle memory in my legs. The runner's high and the thrill of crossing that finish line was buried. Instead, I was weighed down by the thoughts of how hard training for a race was and how crazy I was to think I was a runner. What was once an easy warm-up just a few months ago left me feeling as though I might actually die. In simple terms, starting over sucks. That doesn't mean you shouldn't do it, but just know without a doubt, it isn't easy.

There came a moment in March when I wanted to quit. Okay, truth be told, there were many moments I wanted to quit. There was no shame in quitting at this point. I had already proven to myself I could run a race. Nobody other than my immediate family knew I was training. It would have been really easy to walk away. But I didn't. Instead, I played into my insecurities, and posted on Facebook for all my friends to see, that I was training again. Yep. If you can't talk yourself off the ledge, just jump.

I knew what would happen. I knew as soon as I put out in the world that I was training, my ego wouldn't let me quit. I'm a lot of things, including a horrible runner. But, I'm not a quitter. So I put it on Facebook. After all, if it's on the internet, it has to be true, right?

This simple act meant no turning back. Sure, I sidewinded my training over the next few months. Mega snowstorms and a garage sale treadmill were partially to blame. It didn't matter. I kept showing up. I kept training. Life got busy. I never lost weight. But, I knew in my heart I'd finish strong. And guess what? I did. I set a new PR. It was nowhere near my goal of clearing three hours for a half, but it was a new PR for me.

My favorite racing moment? I ascended one of the steep hills in Peninsula State Park, in Door County, Wisconsin. Winded, I finally reached the crest of the ascent. I heard echoes from a loudspeaker in the distance. As I caught my breath and kept pushing myself forward, I heard them announce the winners. The medal ceremony was already underway. I looked at the lone, fellow back-of-the-pack runner near me and said, "guess we didn't win this one, right?" Or, did we?

Further down the race course, finishers approached me doing their cooldown by running the course backwards. They flooded me with words of encouragement, and I knew the end was near. I crossed the finish line and plopped in the grass, exhausted but feeling accomplished. My husband snapped the sweaty, but necessary, documentation of the moment. I posted it on Facebook and immediately began thinking, "what's next? Imagine what I could do if I trained harder…" And so it began all over again…

Tips for Plotting Your Next Adventure

My favorite part about running (other than buying things) is plotting my next racing adventure. Who doesn't like to dream big?

It's easy to get overwhelmed or say, "I'll just train for something in the fall", and leave it at that. If you are as motivation-challenged as me, the number-one piece of advice I can provide is to be super-specific in your planning. Schedule something on the calendar and make a financial investment – even if it's a year away – within a week of your race. Sometimes, I do this during my taper week just to ensure I don't lose momentum.

Choosing your next adventure can be overwhelming. I've found a very unscientific method that's super-simple. Look at your calendar and choose the season you want to do your next race. For me, that was always spring or fall. My logic stemmed from the fact that I hate running in the heat or sub-zero temperatures. What took me years to realize, though, is that if you run a fall race, your training will encompass all of summer, and a spring race means you'll be starting to train in January. This isn't ideal in northern Wisconsin. But I digress. An equally important factor is the length of the race. Be honest with yourself but aim high. You can always downgrade your goals, but don't tell yourself that you'll sign up for the 5k, and if training is really going well, you'll do the half.

These factors alone will eliminate up to 60% of your race options. From there, pick a region – or regions – you want to visit. I love to make race events a three-day weekend and spend at least one day playing tourist. Running is a great excuse to get your husband to go artisan cheese shopping in Door County or mini golfing in

Minocqua. Last but not least, before you even start to search, be honest with your-self about the size of race you want to run. If you know without a doubt that people aren't your thing, don't register for an urban adventure with 30,000 people.

Once you have your parameters, the fun begins. Start Googling. There are tons of great websites that summarize all of the races in a state. My personal favorite is *run-ningintheusa.com*. Make a list. Which races sound interesting? Just be sure to stick to your season and length. You've chosen those for a reason, and while another race may seem cool, if your calendar and your heart don't align with it, you may be destined to fail. Once you've decided on a race, take a step in solidifying your plan. Register. Book a non-refundable hotel room. Post it on Facebook. Whatever will help you commit to moving forward in your journey.

One quick note: this doesn't preclude you from adding in an extra race. More than once, I've trained for a fall half marathon with no intention of doing any other races, only to find myself lining up at a starting line for a 10k a few weeks before or after it. Those races are an added bonus to my medal rack, but would never happen if I didn't have a plan in place months in advance for another race.

Freedom & Fury
by Carrie Okey

Have you ever won an award for coming in dead last? This is one of my first running memories, from my 6th-grade cross country team, and it still makes me cringe at age 44. (Seriously?! What were those coaches thinking?) Realizing a significant lack of talent for running fast was a blow to my 11-year-old ego, but there was something bigger that kept me from quitting the team – at least for that year. The feel of my sneakers on the rolling fields next to the woods near our middle school course made me feel fast and worthy, despite trailing behind everyone on my team and almost everyone on the other teams who came to race us. I discovered that freedom doesn't come from winning first place. It comes from being steadfast and moving your body forward, unwaveringly.

The track behind my high school is shadowed in darkness and a certain type of despair. It's 7 PM or 9 PM, or sometimes even midnight, when I head there for one of my weekly therapy sessions. I leave my running clothes and shoes in my Polynesian green Geo Metro so I'll be ready when the bank where I work as a teller closes, or the movie I attend with friends is over. I'm 16, and then 17, and trying to fit in, in this busy Chicago suburb. I'm running to change my shape and to hopefully fit the ideal body image that the American media blasts at every girl from cradle to grave. Instead, after the first quarter-mile lap, I find a type of teenage freedom. The fear of being alone in the dark subsides, I stop thinking about what I lack or the pounds I want to lose, and I own my body again. My legs and arms find their rhythm, pumping together and calming my wildly beating heart. There is no loneliness. I fit in with the night sky, the light breeze, and the unspoken truths of the universe.

I am exhausted, out of shape, defeated, and in serious need of an escape. I have two little boys at home and know I need to make the most difficult decision of my life, to leave their dad. Running calls to me, offering me freedom and somewhere to displace the fury that's building inside my chest. It's also a safe place to spend an hour away from my world with no judgment. Look, it's a new mom taking care of herself and getting some exercise. Oh, what a ruse! It's my 11-year-old self, my 17-year-old self, and my now-30-year-old self joining forces to find a way forward, minimizing the hurt to those around me and also to myself. I start running again, downhill and slowly, just one mile. I add hills, more miles, and I work my way up to a half marathon and a medal. Here is the one area of my life where I am winning and I feel free.

Running has been my constant partner throughout the years. I never got fast, but I did find a well of endurance, which has proven way more meaningful to me. A few years ago I discovered another, and perhaps the most significant reason, that I run and run and run. After attending a Younique Foundation retreat for survivors of childhood trauma I learned that when someone experiences trauma at an early age, and they can't escape the abuse by fighting or fleeing, their body retains the feeling of helplessness. Bessel Van Der Kolk, M.D., shares his research on this as well, concerning ways to heal, in his groundbreaking book, *"The Body Keeps the Score"*. For years my body has worked to settle the score, to free me from feeling helpless, unable to escape. It turns out that I wasn't running toward a beauty ideal or an inevitable divorce, I was running to show my little girl-self that I could. And I did! Running has been part of my healing journey for thirty-plus years and I have no doubt it will continue in this role for the next thirty years.

Chapter Eight

Comeback Kid

A funny thing happened the last time I started half marathon training. My boobs hurt. As in, really hurt. At first, I thought that I'd jumped into training too hard. But, as the days progressed and the spasms in my boobs grew more frequent, I knew something was up. I was broken.

It wasn't just my boobs. I was exhausted. I was exhausted when I ran and when I didn't run. I was tired all day long and had no desire to get up in the morning. Granted, it was January in northern Wisconsin. It's hard to be motivated about anything during this dark, sub-zero stretch of hell we call winter. But this was different.

After several weeks of enduring this excruciating pain, I decided to take a break from running for a few days. I thought maybe if I reset myself and started over it'd get better. Only it didn't. It kept getting worse. I didn't know what to do anymore. So I shared my discomfort with my husband. He sort of looked at me perplexed and then asked a very simple but loaded question, "You aren't pregnant, are you?"

I could have smacked him. Of course I wasn't pregnant. I would know if I was pregnant. After all, I'd gone through years of trying to get pregnant. I'd undergone countless fertility tests, prayed to higher powers and visited multiple doctors. While my diagnosis wasn't dire, I clearly didn't get pregnant. We had just gone through a year of paperwork and additional tests to get approved to adopt in the state of Wisconsin. Just a few months prior, we had our hearts ripped from our chests when our birth mom changed her mind about adoption on her way to the hospital. So yes. This was in fact an extremely loaded question. And, of course I wasn't pregnant. Or... was I?

My mind began racing. I had a stash of pregnancy test strips under the sink. It'd be quite simple to do a quick test and put this rumor to rest. But a big part of me didn't want to get my hopes up. I started to do the math in my head. Yes, my period was late. But, if I were a gambler, I'd be broke if I bet on the dates my period would hit. Sometimes it'd be weeks, other times months. Plus, with the stress of the holidays, it'd make sense I was late, right?

After several rounds of inner conversation that was slowly making me crazy, I decide to take a test. I've got nothing to lose. At least then I can rule out this particular crazy notion. I take the test. After a few minutes I glance at the test strip. I see a couple of lines and dismiss the notion. I knew I wasn't pregnant.

Later that night, while nursing my sore boobs, I suddenly found my heart racing. I return to the bathroom and dig the test strip out of the garbage. Two lines. Is it possible that meant I was pregnant? I dig under the sink for the directions. They're missing. I start to panic. How can I not remember if two or three lines mean I'm pregnant?!?!?!

Before you consider me a very dumb blond, remember the circumstances. Factor in that I had purchased these test strips three years ago in bulk on Amazon. They didn't come in a pretty box. These strips didn't have smiley faces or pink lines. They were test strips with multiple faint lines.

I immediately turn to Google looking for answers. After finding the directions online, my life changes in an instant.

"Honey..."

"Yeah?"

"I think I might be pregnant."

Silence. I can hear my husband carefully formulating a sentence in his brain before speaking, knowing the next words he speaks count.

"What do you mean you think you might be pregnant?"

"Well, this test says I'm pregnant, I think."

"You think? Isn't it a yes or a no?"

"Well sort of. But I'm guessing this test is expired."

And so begins the next 24-hours of chaos. My husband runs to the only spot in town to get a test. At the local grocery store, he casually asks the clerk for a pregnancy test. She's ecstatic. She even checks the expiration date to make sure the test is good. Meantime, I'm at home Googling what can cause a false positive. It'd appear that a rare form of cancer and a lot of urban myths are the only options. The sparkling optimist in me becomes convinced that I have cancer.

My husband returns home. "Well, either everyone in town tomorrow will know you're pregnant, or a rumor will be floating around that I'm having an affair." The joys of small-town living.

I begin guzzling water. Lots and lots of water. Three tests later, I'm starting to come to terms with the idea that I may, in fact, be pregnant. My husband is beaming and totally convinced this is the only possibility. I'd like to believe this miracle is real, but the pessimist in me refuses. I need scientific proof. Luckily, I have an awesome doctor and work at a rural hospital that can do same-day appointments.

Less than 24 hours later, I find myself lying on an ultrasound table at work, hearing a rapid pitter-patter, for the first time. It turns out that there actually was a logical explanation besides cancer for the nagging pain in my chest. His name is Jacob William Probst. At the time, I was six weeks pregnant.

Over the course of the next few months, I haphazardly continue my race training schedule. Eventually, I concede that a race isn't in the cards for me until after I give birth. By March, I abandoned running for long walks, occasional dance-offs with my WII and swimming. It's about this same time that an article in the local newspaper confirms that I'm not the only crazy pregnant woman out there.

In Duluth, a woman who was training for a half marathon experiences back pain after running about nine miles. It turns out she is in labor. She gives birth a few days later. This really happens, during the time of my pregnancy. For the record, I never ran nine miles when I was pregnant. Also for the record, I didn't know I was pregnant at first, but there was no way I could have run nine miles prior to going into labor. Reading her story makes me feel like a total loser for quitting my training. Regardless, I quit training.

But now, Jake is born. He's actually five months old. The pregnancy gut is starting to diminish, but I find that I'm weak and exhausted at all times. I need to do something to get back in shape. In terms of weight, I'm actually where I was pre-pregnancy. Keep in mind, this is extremely overweight, but at least I'm not moving backward. Still, I don't feel healthy. So, like any crazy person, I decide to run a half marathon.

I wait until January 1. It is exactly one year after the last time I started training for a half marathon. Similar to last time, I am one hundred percent confident that I'm not pregnant. And, while everything hurts, the pain in my boobs is minimal. As for my back… well that's a different story.

If you've ever tried running post-pregnancy, you'll be familiar with what I'm talking about. Unless, of course, you listen to those wiser than you and actually do things like pilates and yoga while pregnant to ensure you don't lose all of your core strength. While I occasionally dabbled in these exercises, I certainly wasn't consistent. I certainly hadn't maintained any core strength. I was also on bedrest the last four weeks of my pregnancy. It turns out that zero core strength and a hiatus in exercise is a bad foundation to build from when you start running again.

I slowly regroup. The next fifteen weeks are a living hell. While I haven't gained weight, I still have a substantial pregnancy gut. It turns out that despite my best intentions to exercise during pregnancy, my leg muscles are weak at best. Early on in my training, I injure my foot. It's a minor injury and not enough to justify abandoning training.

My child is in daycare, resulting in every germ in northern Bayfield County coming into my home. I endure two chest colds that linger for more than four weeks. I'm knocked out by a stomach bug that leaves me weak and dehydrated.

It turns out the whole "mom" thing is physically, mentally and emotionally exhausting. I have no desire to eat right. I do refrain from eating entire pizzas prior to running, though. I discover how unpleasant teething can be for both baby and mom.

Then there's the weather. It's the winter of 2014. A polar vortex hits northern Wisconsin leaving record-breaking snow and cold. I don't get a chance for my first outside run until a mere three weeks before the race. The week before the race, an April snowstorm dumps enough miserable, white, slush that I start to wonder if I'll be running in pack boots instead of shoes.

Despite these obstacles, I find myself continuously showing up for my dreaded treadmill runs. As for why, I'm not sure. Perhaps the pain is a brief escape from the hormonal tornado of motherhood. It might be that I just need to prove something to myself: that while being a mother has changed my life, I'm still in control of my destiny. It might be that even while my son doesn't understand it quite yet, I want him to know I'm not a quitter. Or, perhaps it's the fact that I'm a stupid, stubborn Finlander who doesn't know how to quit when she's ahead.

In April, I line up for a half marathon in Nisswa, Minnesota. Race organizers claim it is one of the most beautiful races in the state. It weaves around the Brainerd Lakes area. A topography map is never made available to runners. Instead, the website claims there is only a minor elevation change between the start and finish of the race. Foolish me believes that to mean that the course is relatively flat.

Come race day, I'm surprised on many levels. This is my first experience on an open course. My race begins with fighting the 10K racers who start a mere fifteen minutes after me and are irritated by my presence on their course. This is followed by my first adventure on an open course where I often find myself holding my breath as cars whiz by, in the hope of not passing out from their fumes or getting hit. The course does follow the shoreline of several lakes, but I rarely see them given the massive homes plopped between the lake and the endless stretch of residential roads I run. Cheering is scant. The disdain of local residents as my post-pregnant ass waddles by disheartens me. My hope of a relatively flat course diminishes after about the tenth rolling hill on the course. But I keep running. I'm soon lapped by the front-runners in the full marathon. They're on their second round of the course. They're the kindest—shouting words of encouragement as they blast me at the speed of light.

I eventually finish. As I cross the finish line, I'm physically and mentally exhausted. I come in second-to-last place. I don't feel accomplished or proud of today's achievement until I see my husband grinning at me. He knows what today means to me. He understands that this wasn't just a race in which winning was measured in PRs or split times. This was my comeback.

Tips on Making a Comeback

For me, running as a new mama was as equally challenging as rewarding. It wasn't just the extra weight or sleep deprivation that got to me, though. It was mama guilt. You know what I'm talking about. That deep-seated societal pressure that's put on us that leaves us believing that if we do anything for ourselves, we're letting our newborn down. I mean, in what other country would a point of pride be placed on how many days you haven't showered or slept while caring for your child?

I was blessed to have an extremely supportive husband. He wanted me to get out and his work and social schedule reflected that. If I ever wanted to hit the open road, he'd gladly hold the door for me. But, as soon as I left, I'd start filling my head with the nonsense of wondering what kind of new mom I was, training for a half marathon right after my son was born? I already had the "I'm going back to work full-time" strike against me as well.

Equally stressful was the fact that I'm not one of those folks that dreams about running. If you gave me a choice between chilling on the couch reading a great book, hiking in the woods, completing an MBA online, or running, running would easily come in last. Don't get me wrong, I've always loved running, after a good run. Or when shopping for accessories or shoes or watching inspirational videos. But that's distinct from the actual act of running.

Overcoming mama guilt and not being a motivated runner are two major obstacles I still struggle to overcome. As if that isn't enough, there's a third obstacle that's almost more of an impediment: the simple words *have to* versus *get to*. My husband doesn't understand my running but supports it. He considers it my hobby and a way for me to spend some quality time in the woods with myself. I, on the other hand, consider it a chore. And in my house, chores do not count as quality downtime.

I'm not sure how time is divided up in your home, but in ours we make an effort to give each other quality alone-time each weekend. This is often sandwiched between quality couple-time, quality family-time, more quality couple-time and household duties. This means that if I go mow the lawn, that's considered a household duty, not me pursuing my life's passion. This system worked really well, right up until Jake. Before Jake arrived on the scene, it was easy to allocate some quality couple time and spend the rest of the weekend pursuing our dreams and splitting household chores. After Jake, not so much. And, while I told my husband I loved running, I meant it more in the metaphorical sense of things.

If I'm being honest, for a long time, running was comparable to mowing my lawn. It's a means to an end. I absolutely love a freshly mowed lawn, much as I enjoy crossing a finish line, but the actual act of mowing, not so much. The same rings true for running. I need a lot of motivation to hit the road. I never really enjoyed it. And, as any chore, I started to resent my runs. I'd come home tired and sweaty and want nothing more than to crash on the couch and binge-watch a show. Instead, my husband would be patiently awaiting my arrival so he could go pursue his hobbies. Guess what? This is not a recipe for success, folk.

Now, I try to look at the training runs as a gift to myself. I try to save my favorite podcasts to enjoy in the woods. In the winter, I savor certain tv shows from the comfort of my treadmill. I try to tell myself that I don't have to run, but instead I get to run. Does it always work? Um, no. I'm batting maybe a twenty percent success rate. But that's better than zero. I'm also honest with myself about the fact that running is just one of many things that are important to me, so my life needs to reflect that. I can't spend fifteen weeks of my precious leisure time training to the point where I hate running and am only doing it because I'm not a quitter. At the same time, it also means I'm probably never going to complete a full marathon or hit my half marathon goal time, because I'm not willing to do the work. It does mean I can still do half marathons and enjoy shorter races at a reasonable pace for me. That was a big shift for me, but it was an important one.

On a more practical level, after Jake was born I got the book *Run Like a Mother: How to get moving—and not lose your family, job or sanity*. This book is packed with practical advice and tips on how to run before, during and after pregnancy, not to mention plenty of inspiration from other moms. The authors Dimity McDowell and Sarah Bowen Shea are both mothers themselves, which I think is an important distinction in understanding the realities of putting yourself first in a shifting family dynamic. The book came out in 2010, and since then, they've also launched a podcast and online community called Another Mother Runner. Both of these are great tools for new and old moms. I learn something regularly from this community.

Chapter Nine

Incentives

Always earned, never given. For Valentine's Day, my hubby bought me this quote as a metal hanger for my medals. At the time, I was super-excited about adding another medal to the mix. I was at the height of training for my fifth half marathon but I was only averaging three-to-five mile runs, making it somewhat easy and enjoyable. By mid-April, the novelty of training had worn off and I was left looking at that rack and a month of long runs, wondering what the hell I was thinking.

The race was slated for early spring – Mother's Day weekend to be exact. In northern Wisconsin. The race itself is called Journey's and takes place near Minocqua. This is tourism country at its finest, but in what we lovingly call "shoulder season" here. As in, the time nobody really wants to visit so you create events in hopes to fill hotels. For me, I love this time of year and if given a choice will take bad weather in shoulder season above hot weather and overcrowded spaces during peak tourism. But this also meant training in a lot of snow or on treadmills. Both of which I hate. Nevertheless, I cobbled together a training plan and did the best I could.

Two weeks prior to race day I did a trial run. It was clear that despite having a longer training time, I wasn't going to come anywhere close to my goal. To be honest, I was pretty disappointed in myself. I felt I had a solid plan and was determined to clear three hours. But looking back, I didn't diet or push myself early on to improve my time. And the reality is, if you change nothing about your training you can pretty much expect the same results. That's the hard truth about running. You get out exactly what you put in.

For some, running is about setting a very specific goal – often time-related. For those folks, they can refer to any of the hundreds of training, diet and mental health plans available to help them achieve those goals. For those with discipline, barring any major injuries or illness, the roadmap to training is pretty solid. But, let's be frank for a moment. I'm someone who oozes determination and discipline in a lot of areas of my life. I'm a first-generation college student who, over the course of Twenty years has successfully completed various degrees four times, all while addressing other major milestones in life like dating, marriage, being a caregiver and motherhood. I set career goals, gardening goals, and vision-cast myself into a life I always dreamed of. All that said, when it comes to the discipline required for running, it just isn't there. My intentions are there, I always train enough to ensure that my toenails remain intact, and I don't actually jeopardize my health by shocking my heart with an abrupt transition from the couch to a half marathon. I also eat all the food. I binge-watch the shows. I float around my lake on a floatie as opposed to swimming it. I drive instead of bike. I purchase smoothies, only to have them collect freezer burn, at the same time that I purchase glazed donuts and rationalize eating two instead of one because we wouldn't want the donuts to go to waste, right?

But I keep showing up. To do this, I channel my inner Sisu – the grit and determination of a hard-core Finlander. I also channel my inner materialist by investing in plenty of unnecessary but fun gadgets and gizmos that provide the incentive needed to haul my ass out of bed at five am for an early morning, black fly-plagued run in 90% humidity. For those who live in northern Wisconsin, you know exactly the type of mornings I'm talking about. For those who don't, just picture your definition of Hell and double it.

I've bribed myself with a lot of prizes over the years. Early on, my husband used to pay my entrance fees. Sometimes I'd piggyback trips around a race, making a morning race into a five-day vacation. I've devoured entire bags of chips, fresh-baked bread and specialty cheeses. This coupled with a strong why and my stubborn attitude is what makes me cross the finish line. My why or just being stubborn isn't enough on their own. Instead, I've found these prizes help, folks. Perhaps that makes me shallow. I'd much rather be a shallow individual sporting a new running top and a medal than sitting on the couch unmotivated and not running.

These fun superficial accessories have helped me more than anyone will ever know. They've powered me through running slumps and given me confidence to show up at the starting line. By 2015, I was a few races post-baby and still trying to balance running, motherhood and a career. I was, and still am, that plus-size girl in the back.

Race day eve I hit up the health expo. The Journey's race has some great swag, including entertaining bondibands that mock the sheer and utter craziness of running a race. I grabbed a few free items and headed to the cabin my family had booked for the weekend to attempt to relax. It didn't work. By nightfall, I just wanted the race to be over. By race day morning, my stomach hurt. Not because of race day jitters, but just frustration. To add to this joy, I had the pleasure of being the larger-than-average gal lining up with a bunch of skinny runners. Don't shake your head at me and say, "but you are a runner." You know what I'm talking about. If you want to feel fat, head to a half marathon and look at those in your company. It was during my time in the port-a-potty line that I noticed something distinctly different about this race. It was my mindset. As I patiently waited for my turn to unload, I decided to quit dwelling on what I didn't do and acknowledge the fact that in fifteen minutes I was going to line up and run a race. And sometime in the next four hours I'd finish the race. What I made of the time in between was up to me. Yes, I could dwell on what I didn't do. But I could also say, "I'm still here and why not enjoy today?"

And I did. Maybe enjoy is the wrong word, since I was in intense pain. But I can honestly say I had fun. The Journey's Half Marathon in Eagle River/Minaqua area was a turning point for me, in terms of moving my mentality from asking, "Am I going to die?" to "how hard can I push myself?" Somewhere around mile six with the tune, "This is my Fight Song" playing (thank you for sharing the song, Courtney!), I really started pushing myself. I pushed myself harder than I'd ever have done before running. By mile twelve, I was wondering if I'd pushed too hard. Whether I'd actually clear the finish line before collapsing. But I did. Later, when I checked my time, I discovered my time was 3:13. In runner's time, that meant I missed my goal by a lifetime. But in my time, that was fifteen minutes faster than my last race and twenty-five minutes faster than my first run. More importantly, I put it all out there on the race course and discovered I have a lot more in me that I thought possible. The icing on the cake was seeing my son when I finished and knowing that someday he'll understand that while his mom might not finish first, she finishes what she starts and tries her hardest. And for right now, that's enough.

My motivators

The best advice I can give on this is to set a budget early on and then plan to double it. If incentives are what it takes to finish your training, this is an investment not worth skimping on. I think of my friends who have spent hundreds on gym memberships or workout clothes or even running shoes, only to never use them, and well, what's the point in that? Is it better to spend $150 on shoes and then another $150 on incentives to make sure you use the shoes and actually show up for the starting line or to cut your losses at $150 and give up? I'll choose the $300 every time.

Earlier in this book, I talked about running necessities. This is about running incentives. This isn't so much about function, as it is fashion, or making a statement. Or showing that you belong to a tribe which, even if you hate running, is a point of pride for you. It's also about pampering yourself and allowing yourself to acknowledge what a badass you're becoming.

Topping that list: pedicures. I didn't grow up getting pedicures. In fact, my first pedicure came during my running exploits. My first (and only) manicure was the day before I got married. Pedicures always seemed like an overpriced luxury that rich people indulged in. It wasn't until I was gifted one prior to a race that I realized what an incredible, worthwhile investment this sixty minutes of pampering can be, both to my soul and my tired calves and feet. Most of the time I go with blue nails, because that's my signature color, but really, I could care less about the color. It's the massaging and the scrubbing and the sloughing that is sheer and utter bliss. On a side note, I also invested in a PedEgg. This tool grosses my husband out, but callouses are a rough reality of running and there is something very satisfying about removing layers of hardened skin from your heels. It's a definite must-have at home.

Outside of pedicures, there's the post-run latte. I'm a serious coffee lover. I also live in rural Wisconsin where the nearest year-round coffee shop is over thirty minutes away. More than once, I've either driven that far to run, so that my cool-down could entail walking into an independent shop and buying the largest cup of caffeine-charged steamed milk possible. In the summer months, I've strategically ended my long double-digit runs at our local shop in town. There, I remove a sweaty $20 bill from my sports bra and order the full-fat, full-sugar latte with just a hint of guilt for wandering in like an unwashed woman coming off an all-night bender. The post-race treats are equally amazing. There's generally a leisurely brunch or promised online purchase that acknowledges my hard work. Occasionally, my husband even gets involved.

A special place to hang medals, gifted to me by my husband, was just the start. I chose the saying Always Earned, Never Given as a reminder that what you put in is what you get out. After many moons of running, I am cool with this. The feeling of liberation that comes with crossing the finish line is enough. The rack hangs in my office.

Then, there are the finisher t-shirts. After a while, you start to wonder what to do with these shirts. I mean, they're rarely shirts you'd wear in public, other than right after the race. And I have my favorite running shirts, so these don't work for that. But donating them? That seems crazy. For years they collected in my closet until I'd accumulated about thirty of them. Now, they've been repurposed to create the most mis-matched, colorful, and meaningful throw quilt I've ever owned. It sits on my couch downstairs and is a great conversation piece. I mean seriously, how cool is it to say, when someone asks about it, "Oh that thing? That's just a quilt of all of my finisher shirts." That's right… while I will never place in a race, I can say that I have a 4x6 quilt of finisher shirts. So there's that. My husband gifted that to me as well.

That's just the tip of the iceberg, though. Every race has swag for sale. Every ache and pain has a solution. Think foam rollers and now the latest rage I'm research-ing – hyper ice. There are the tennis balls you can roll your feet on, car seat towels to capture your perspiration, body glide, compression socks, cell phone holders and the wristband key holder. And the food. Walking through a health expo is like Black Friday for runners. I've never successfully cleared one without some must-have that I either buy that day or add to my next wish list for my husband or my Amazon cart.

Do I believe all of the product claims I encounter? Absolutely not. But when I line up at the start line, do I want to feel like I belong? Absolutely. Do I feel that after all of these years I've earned a sense of belonging in the running tribe? Absolutely. I haven't gone as far as the 13.1 bumper sticker on my car or tattoo on my wrist, but I have no problem telling someone, "oh I'm limping right now because I'm in training." My advice to you is to embrace the tribe. You don't need to buy any of these items to run. But if you're someone who enjoys them, simple items can be pretty cost-effective and help remind you of how far you've come and how much you deserve to celebrate your inner victories. If you want to, just buy the darn shirt and wear it with pride. You've earned it!

The Starting Line
by Roberta King

I never saw the basketball coming. Hard bonk on the shoulder.
I ducked instead of catching the softball. Took it between the eyes.
A missed kickball rolled up my leg. Split my lip.
Balls and me, we don't get along.

I came of age in the mid-1970s, an only child of parents solidly middle class, but slightly older parents. Sport wasn't their thing. My dad was a swimmer, but my mother never expended any sort of physical effort other than walking the Easter Parade in New York City in 1954. My family wasn't sporty.

I tried out for track my junior year in high school because it wasn't a ball sport and unlike other sports at the school, I'd heard we'd be practicing alongside the boy's track team. Bonus.

There were six of us at tryouts and we all made the team. I was proud, regardless of the circumstance. I loved the school-issued tee shirt with my last name, KING, printed on the back in green letters. I anticipated getting my picture taken for the yearbook and being part of a sports team instead of just the student council and school paper. And sweatpants? What could be more comforting for a high school girl than her first pair of sweatpants? I lived in those gray cotton pants.

When the snow melted and we weren't running up the two flights of stairs and down the halls of the school, we went outside for practice. My Christian school didn't have the funds for a track, so our meets were all away, at better-funded Christian schools or the local publics. For our distances we'd run through the neighborhood near the school, the boys leading and us girls following close behind. The boys had a few more years as a track team than we did, that's all. Sometimes our team would divert, making a shortcut around a block, between two houses or down an alley, cutting ahead of the boys. Think smarter when you're not faster.

My real motivation for trying out for the track team (other than the boys) was the coach—the handsome Mr. VerMerris—the school's chemistry and physics teacher (two classes I never took). He was Mark Spitz with salt-and-pepper hair. "He's dreamy," I told my teammate Stacy. For sprinting practice, Mr. VerMerris would stand at the end of a field to the east of the school. All that was between him and me (and thirty other runners) was a couple hundred yards of uneven, picker-laden dead grass and packed sand. With his arms outstretched from his sides and a silver whistle between his perfect white teeth, he gave the signal and we raced toward him. I've never run faster. My legs and arms pumped. I could hear my breathing and feel my heart thumping. I didn't reach Mr. VerMerris first, but I stopped directly in front of him, millimeters from a collision. I don't recall what he said, but his blue eyes sparkled and there was the reward.

We only had three meets that year. I ran the mile. Last place every time. I threw the shot. A good put was twenty feet. I was the middle leg of the 880 relay and our team placed fourth out of eight teams, at one meet. I earned an athletic letter—a small, green, fuzzy C. I sewed it to a jacket that I wore for a few years. I'm proud of that C and kept it when the jacket went to Goodwill.

That was 1976 and I've never stopped running and am a solid middle-pack runner. My personal goal is to finish upright, with a smile, and to be one person above the 50th percentile. I took up the sport of running seriously, as in running races, in 1986. Wherever I travel, I run to sightsee and try to pick up a race where I'm able. I've sweated through a run on a 90-degree September day in Miami and along the Malecon in Havana. I killed my quads running a downhill half marathon in Colorado, twice. I've run big races like the A1A Half in Fort Lauderdale, but my personal preference is races in small towns. Because as a middle-packer, placing in your age group is more likely to happen and medals are sometimes awarded five or more places deep. As an older runner, too, I've outlasted other women in the sport and by age alone might be one of just three or four women in the 60+ age group. Bring on the swag!

Even though running is a solitary sport, I've fostered relationships with women who run and love running. I've been through pre-race-night and morning routines with friends who run—that alone builds an intimacy that lasts a lifetime. No one loves talking about running more than another runner.

I love to run outside year-round and don't mind the weather. Michigan winters bring blowing snow and sub-zero, 10-degree-windchill days along Lake Michigan's shore near my house where I've been splashed by cars in a sleet storm, got knocked off my feet by strong gust of wind and tripped on a chunk of ice, bloodying my knee.

Always, though, when the going gets tough, I think of Mr. VerMerris and I kick it in.

Chapter Ten

My Why

"Why do you keep running if you hate it so much?" my primary medical doctor casually asks me during my annual physical.

"Great question," I respond, thinking in my head that'd be like my therapist asking me if I've figured out the meaning of life.

I get it. It's a legit question. Every time she sees me or my child, the subject of running inevitably comes up. Every time, I talk about it being a means to an end, which leads her to ask me, "wouldn't it be easier to find something you enjoy that is active?" Perhaps. That said, she clearly doesn't know me as well as I know myself.

If you're still reading this book you've probably established that in addition to being fat, I'm stubborn. In some ways, that stubborn mule inside me is preventing me from finding a sport I love. I don't care, though. Because I truly believe the things that change you don't come easy.

Several years into my running routine, the local winery in town decided to sponsor a running group to complete an Insane Inflatable 5k. I didn't think much of it until a few days before the race, when they had someone drop out and asked if I wanted to run. Without hesitation I said, "Sure. Why not?"

Let's pause for a minute and repeat what I said: "Sure, why not?" That's right. Prior to lacing up and sweating my brains out on miles of endless pavement, an ask like that would have sent me into a tailspin. Never mind that it's s an untimed race that roughly equates to a grown-up bouncy house course, and it's meant to be fun. The only thing I would have acknowledged is that fat girls don't run, and therefore on what planet would I sign up for such nonsense?

Instead, my only thought was, "I wonder if there's a medal." That weekend, I lined up with a gaggle of White Winter Winery friends and fans, only a few of whom I'd ever met. We skipped and jumped and bounced our way through those obstacles like nobody's business.

Was I graceful? If you consider an elephant attempting to launch itself over an inflatable wall graceful, sure. I jumped. I bounced. I ran. I laughed... and laughed so hard and so long that I maybe wet myself a little bit. At some point, I stumbled over a finish line and got a simple medal and some beer tickets. I laughed some more and then went about my day with my fam, ending with some of the most fabulous pizza, from Thirsty Pagan in Superior, Wisconsin. It was frankly a perfect day that never would have happened if I hadn't already decided that I've earned the right to show up to these races as much as the next person.

Over the course of my running career, I've had a few opportunities like this. A hilly ski trail run, the early season 5k that involves a bottle opener finishing medal and brunch-style bloody mary's that could feed a small country. There was the time I ran through the tunnels of a closed interstate, or when I experienced both frostbite and sunburn at an early season half marathon that took me so long to finish that I started in snow and ended under hot, sunny blue skies. I even contemplated (until COVID-19 hit) challenging myself to a twelve-hour relay run in Copper Harbor, Michigan just for fun. I've run road races, trail races, flat races, hilly races, big races and small races. I've run with friends and in a sea of strangers. It took me a while, but somewhere along the way, I discovered that I belong there just as much as the next gal. Sure, the magazines and blogs and runner guides may not reflect that (you'll find in most training guides fifteen minute miles is the slowest mile you can run.) Shame on them for excluding me. But, I've finally come to terms with the fact that they can exclude me in the books, but it's ultimately their loss. Because I've earned a spot at that starting line. Even more surprising is the fact that the only person busy judging me on these adventures is me. The running community, in general, is one of the most accepting groups I've ever encountered.

My point is, as much as I hate running, I do love being a runner. I love buying shoes, socks and stretchy black running pants. I love checking out new trails, reading inspirational running stories, posting selfies from gorgeous vistas, and runner swag. I love the running culture—the kind strangers you joke with on the trail or catch a ride with on the shuttle bus. The ultra-fast marathoners who pass me on the trail and take time to tell me I'm doing great, even though they've run more than thirteen miles than me and can run two to three miles to my one.

Now, the logical side of me points out that I could experience many of these things without ever completing a race. Brooks running shoes can be worn on a walk. Stretchy black pants were my weekend-wear long before I hit the open roads. I found Usain Bolt inspiring well before I understood the pain that comes with pushing through the runner wall and discovering you are capable of much more if you just keep moving. Cliché as it may sound, I wouldn't enjoy it nearly as much without the suffering.

I realize that deep down, one of the primary reasons I hate running is because I'm mediocre at it. I'm a mediocre runner because I'm not willing to put the work in to be a good runner. I'm not willing to do the stretches, train regularly, eat healthy and lose weight so that my legs aren't carrying an extra hundred pounds. In other words, I'm mediocre at running because I choose to be mediocre.

Nearly a decade ago, I overcame my insecurities and lined up for my first timed races. I had decided to become a runner after indulging in too many chips and mojitos, waking up hungover and seriously questioning my unmotivated self. I had just gotten borderline news from my primary care doctor that implied that if I wanted to continue indulging in chips, I needed to start moving more. A plus-size gal in my early 30s, several acquaintances raised their brow at me when I declared I was going to be a runner. The only logical response for this Finn was to sign up and complete a half marathon, because the best way to get me to do something is to tell me I can't. My time was slow, but I finished.

But why after nearly a decade of disappointing finishing times do I keep showing up? Why do I continue to show up for a sport that brings out the worst of my athleticism on the best of days?

Something keeps bringing me back to the trail. Perhaps it is my inner Sisu—the gritty hustler deep within me that says I'm running for me and that's enough. It doesn't matter if I'm first or last. Instead, this run reminds me that you get out what you put in. And that at times, that needs to be enough. This is about progress, not perfection, folks.

In all the tangible ways of measuring my running successes, I've failed. Except I haven't failed, because I keep showing up. I'm not willing to let the dream of being a good runner and thoughts of everything I could have or should have done prevent me from being a runner today. I'm not willing to let the part of me that longs to finish first or to be the best prevent me from doing something folks said I couldn't do. Call it cliché, but I run because I can, and for someone who has a one-legged dad, that means something.

Tactical Tip

Nike said it best: just do it. But if that's not enough, here's a reading recommendation that will change your life. It's called *Grit*, by Angela Duckworth. Those who've read the book might question my parallel between mediocrity and Duckworth's explanation of why some people succeed. It all goes back to my why. My why isn't to be the next Kara Goucher. My why is to put myself out there, to immerse myself in a culture that a decade ago I felt didn't include people like me, and continuing to show up, unapologetically, as myself. Even if it's a bit embarrassing and humbling as fuck. Running is not my passion. But defying the odds is, and that's where my grit comes into play.

In *Grit*, Duckworth says, "nobody wants to show you the hours of becoming. They'd rather show the highlight of what they've become."

There are a million books out there by successful runners who share their motivational highs with you. These badass women get up in the morning and want to run. It's their passion and their life, and this shows through all the sacrifices they make (and the phenomenal PRs they run). This is not one of those books. Because as inspiring as those stories are, for every single one of those there is an ordinary gal like me just wanting to cross that finish line and feel the joy that comes from finishing something that she thought she couldn't. A gal that wants to balance cookies and Saturday cocktails, being a mom, working full-time and volunteering in her community with also being a runner and believing that's possible, even if it means finishing last. Ultimately, it's all about perspective, because for every race I finish last, there are thousands of individuals who started to train but didn't believe they had it in them to finish. I know – I was once one of them. And that my friends, is what true grit is about.

Chapter 11

The Running Rut

Remember that runner's high I mentioned after completing my fifth half marathon? I'd like to say that lasted. It didn't. Despite having a great race, I was completely depleted. I walked away from that race elated but also recognizing that it'd be difficult to repeat that performance. I'm not a super serious athlete, but I'm a competitive person by nature. I'm also someone who believes in continuous improvement. This, unfortunately, means, that I'm only as good as my last race. For some, this is a motivator. Often, this theory works well in applied to most areas of my life. But not for running. Instead, it's just one more psychological barrier I need to overcome.

Anyway, this led me to question what would be next and to determine that a half marathon can't be the answer. It was only May, so I knew a fall race was in my cards. It was just a matter of which race. And that's when it dawned on me. Why a half marathon? So I made a decision in that moment to abandon my streak of half marathons for a 10k.

If I'm being really honest, my gut told me that I wasn't motivated enough to even complete a half marathon training schedule, let alone run one. So, a shorter race seemed like less work. It seemed achievable. I could up my mantra of just finishing, to finishing faster. It felt exciting to set some new goals with a new distance. I'm not sure what ultimately pushed me over the edge, but I ultimately signed up for my first 10k.

My first 10k training plan lasted eleven weeks. While it was shorter than my half marathon training, it was equally challenging. Why? Because while the distances were shorter, my biggest barrier to running is always the mind games I play prior to hitting the road. These little buggers don't discriminate and are equally vocal whether I'm doing a fifteen-minute run or a ten-miler. But, here's the crazy thing: I started to enjoy running.

Perhaps it was the magical fall weather we'd been having. Or maybe it was because the shorter runs that comprised this training schedule were a lot more achievable since I'd just come off running a half marathon. Regardless, I can genuinely say that I enjoyed this training. It felt good. So good, in fact, that on a whim I decided to throw a 5k into the mix.

My motivation for this was my little boy, Jake. My race pick: the Birkie Trail

Run. For those who aren't from northern Wisconsin, the Birkie Trail Run is a combination of ultra, relay, marathons and a 5k. It takes place on the Birkebeiner Ski Trail, which hosts the country's largest Nordic ski race. But more importantly, it's also hilly as fuck. When I registered for the race, I didn't really think about the hills. I was focused on the fact that it was half the distance of my 10k, I love the area, and it was going to be a gorgeous day, so why not? It also included a kids race that I thought my son would seriously enjoy. A win-win, right?

Reality check: the Birkie course is solid hills. And if you plan to attempt even a 5k trail run, it would be wise to do at least a couple trail runs (or heck, even a single one!) and perhaps some training on hills. But, whatever. I had a blast. I walked as-needed and found that I finished in a decent time, by my standards, given the circumstances. More importantly, I didn't injure myself.

I also had enough gas in my tank to immediately run another 1k with my son, right after my race. It was one of those perfect all days and Jake was on fire. Sure, he didn't cross the finish line first. But like mom, he gave it everything he had and crossed the finish line with pride. He also got a sweet pair of socks out of the deal. Afterward, we enjoyed some of my favorite pizza in the world at River's Eatery in Cable, Wisconsin. This isn't an ad placement, but seriously: best pizza on the planet! I left that day, realizing that this is what people who love running must feel when they hit the course. I'm not that kind of person, generally, but looking back, it was one of my most joyful running days.

Equally important: the race reminded me that in running, you reap what you sow. You really do get back what you put in. It also fueled me to complete my last few weeks of training honestly. I really did the work. Interval training, long runs, and proper nutrition. I even threw in a few stretches. By race day, I knew I was ready. At that point, my mindset was: half the length, half the work (this was not true.) I knew I could run 13.1 miles, so I couldn't even rationalize the idea that I might not finish. And remember, my mantra is to finish strong.

Come race day, I was blessed with cloudy skies but no rain. It was a humid day, but not overly hot. It was definitely a blessing compared to my spring half. Plus, I only had 6.2 miles to go this time. Don't get me wrong, running 6.2 miles – or any miles – at my size doesn't come naturally or easily. But in my mind it seemed much easier than a half marathon.

I somehow missed the start of the race. I was chatting with a co-worker and frankly just lost track of time. It didn't really matter, since my time didn't start until I crossed the marker. And with no time for nerves or stretching, I had no choice but to just push forward. Given the shorter time on the course, I removed all of my favorite love songs and country ballads from my playlist, leaving only upbeat bubblegum pop songs, the occasional rap (Baby Got Back) song and plenty of toe-stomping country tunes. Surprisingly, this type of music can really carry you through a race. Anyway, it was an uneventful race except for the fact that I ran. That's right. I always considered that fifteen-minute miles was sort of my tipping point. Slower than that, it was more of a waddle-jog. Faster averages meant I was actually running. This race, all of my miles were under fourteen minutes. Granted, this was my first 10k and I had no PR to compare it to, but it was substantially better than the 15:49 per mile pace I executed in one of my worst half marathons ever, the previous spring. It almost had to be.

My goal was to finish in 1:30 and I managed to do it in 1:26:02. For me, that felt pretty awesome. I learned a lot in this race – not so much about my personal will-power, but rather my potential as a runner. Somewhere after crossing that finish line, I found I could finally say I felt like an actual runner. Perhaps a slow runner, but not a jogger or waddler; just a novice runner trying to find her way in a sea of spandex. At the finish, my son yammered on about how "mommy ran super fast!" and he gave me the biggest hug, ever. If that doesn't make you feel like a superhero, I'm not sure what else it'd take.

The Running Mix

At some point in your running career, you'll find yourself wanting to mix things up. For me, it came when the thought of starting another fifteen weeks of week-end-long runs left me nauseated. I wasn't interested in investing every Saturday, August through October, to black fly, sweat-drenched runs. My heart and gut screamed "NOOO!" My resounding sentiment made it clear that no pair of fancy shoes or pedicure would carry me through this training season.

The great thing, though, is if you're reading this book, it isn't because you want to pursue a professional running career for which you have to train. The best advice I can give you is to ask yourself, from the comfort of your couch, *what am I trying to accomplish?*

In the beginning, I really wanted to finish a half marathon because some outside force (and inner voice) was implying I couldn't. My motivation was to give the world (and my insecurities) the finger. But as time went on, it became more about a voice in my mind that said, *I wonder if…*

For years, *wonder if…* was a sentiment I only explored in the context of half marathons. There came a point, though, when the thought of training for one more half marathon might have killed me. It certainly would have decimated any remaining running spirit I had in me. It was then that I realized that there are thousands of other races in my region, and rather than beat myself up, I could just try something else.

It sounds super simple. I'm not winning any points with my brilliance and insight here. But this advice matters. When the running rut happens, change it up. Change your distance. Change the type of course. Change your training plan. Buy different shoes. Create a new playlist. Try running without music. Wear shorts. Wear pants. Invest in extra-strength deet or use a new sunscreen. Run with a new friend. Run alone. Try running and smiling. Or swinging your arms around like a boxer/back-up dancer while attempting to channel your inner badass self as you run short sprints in front of your house. Just MIX IT UP.

It's crazy how signing up for that 10k motivated me to keep running. It gave me the space to continue running for all of the reasons I loved running, while also allowing me to pursue other passions (like writing this book). Like everything in life, running has seasons. Acknowledge those and adjust accordingly. It would've been all too easy to convince myself that I didn't have time for a half and to walk away from the entire running scene. But after the resounding "NOOO!" I registered at the thought of training for a half, there was also a quiet "yesss!" telling me that I wasn't ready to walk away from running. I just needed a change of scenery.

Tami's Story

I Get Knocked Down... But I Get Up Again
By Tami Unseth

In 2014, I decided to participate in a two-mile walk/run fundraiser for our local library. I came in first place. What a rush! And so, my running journey began: a journey I never thought or imagined I would pursue. You see, a year prior I was paralyzed from the waist down, from a fall that doctors said "crimped the wires in my spinal column".

The injuries didn't stop there. In the early part of May 2015, I ended up tearing my ACL in two while participating in a FUN inflatable 5k race in Superior, with friends. Go figure. I surprised myself at how much this bothered me. I was devastated. Surgery was in June, and come the end of August, I completed a 5k race (walking, of course). I was not done; I was getting back after it.

I started running about four to six times a week and found myself registering for at least a race or two a month. I was on a roll! My endurance and my speed were slowly increasing, and fat was starting to melt. My first half marathon was mid-October in 2016, and I opted for a training plan from Hal Higdon that I had found on the internet. The training plan increased mileage each week and was not focused on speed at all. I structured some strength and cross-training into my non-run days, again. I did, however, make sure I was completing the scheduled mileage, no matter what was going on. I also joined a few Facebook running groups for inspiration, advice, suggestions and camaraderie. I acquired a lot of knowledge regarding running form, pace, speed, intervals, tempos, various styles/makes of shoes, clothing, bladder vests, running watches, and other accessories to help one along their journey.

During preparation for my first half, I endured a lot of bad runs in which my legs, body, stomach, and even my brain, felt like they were not in agreement at all. That was definitely frustrating, and at times, it was a setback for me. I struggled greatly with accepting that these bad runs were okay, even needed, during my journey. I sure did learn a lot about myself. Nonetheless, the day came for my first half marathon. And I did it! I really did it! Oh, what a fabulous feeling! I cried so many happy tears. Savor the rush you get after conquering a goal. Shortly afterward, I signed up for another half marathon.

My second half marathon was scheduled for May of 2017. Winter training was a chore – a lot of treadmill running. I'm not a huge fan of that option. But come race day, I PR'd by almost 20 minutes and was ecstatic! I felt like Wonder Woman; there was no stopping me! Flying on my "runners high", I ended up pushing myself to complete at least one race every month. But... injuries returned. This time a hip issue flared up, slowing down my time and forcing me to downgrade my intended-first marathon to a walking half marathon.

Yep. I had taken the leap and signed up for my first full marathon, to take place October of 2017, one year after my first half. I tried again the following year, signing up for yet another full, that ended up being downgraded to walking the half again. This time the alteration in plans was due to a mild stroke that I suffered on Memorial Day in 2018. So dang discouraging. I even entertained thoughts that maybe I should just give up and find another outlet. After a little over two weeks in the hospital, and a few months at home, and weighing in at almost 200 pounds, I had regained full use of my left side and was released to go about my daily life as I pleased. I found myself missing the feeling I would get from running. So, I registered for more races and set forth training... again. When you get knocked down, you stand back up again. Onward.

I signed up for a full marathon – the same one I had been shooting for: WhistleStop 2019. The next chapter of my running journey, I played it safe and smart, as I continue to do today. I journaled, read books and blogs, listened to some podcasts and made a few good friends who run. Running had become a part of me again. It's still a physical and mental struggle, at times, but it's one I'm focused on. I'm improving greatly, though the struggle is so real. I remind myself that I'm doing good and moving forward. That this is starting over, and I can't compare my current standards with my previous races, times, paces, or anything that I was doing prior to the stroke. Now is my new beginning, and I face it stronger than before.

I followed Hal Higdon's marathon plan for the most part. The mileage increased during weekdays, which was a struggle for me. I'd taken on a travel contract job in another state and was on my own. But I was up for the challenge. I would make sure I ended at home, or my husband came to my finish location, for my long week-end-runs, just so I wasn't alone. During the week, I would get up early in the morning and get the miles done before work. It was a struggle at first, but running at 5 a.m. eventually became a welcome routine for the summer. When it stopped being light out at 5 AM, I opted for the local YMCA treadmill to get my mileage in. When the weekday miles exceeded four, I'd divide them between early morning treadmill and evening treadmill sessions, and outside runs, depending on when I was done with work.

I tried a variety of foods for the night before, and morning of, a long run, to determine what worked best for me. I was a nervous wreck the eve of the race and hardly slept. I ran the first half a bit too strong feeling great at the time. This was not a smart move on my part. By mile thirteen, my body started aching in various places, and weirdly, my feet were hurting. This continued through the entire second half of the race. My pace decreased drastically, walking intervals became longer, and I started limping, through tears. My goals were: to not be the last runner across the finish line, and to cross the finish line under the six-hour cut-off mark. I kept reminding myself of those goals and talking to myself, even out loud (it wasn't as if anyone was near me, at this point.) I finished the race and reached both goals, with the help of a good friend along the last mile. Everyone was pretty much gone by the time I finished, other than my small crowd of supporters, at the finish line. Boy, did I cry and hurt.

Running is still my outlet, my therapy, my escape. I continue to run and register for as many races and distances as I can, as long as my body lets me. Yes, there are good and bad runs, just like anything else in our lives. You take them as they come and make the best of it. The bad runs provide lessons that you learn from. You learn what your body can do, and what your mind can do. You also learn that attitude and stress play a huge part in how well you run and how your body adapts. Some people say that they run to alleviate stress, and it does help, but if you are looking for a PR, you definitely don't want to be running with a bad attitude or much negativity built up inside; it will deter you from your goals. Running is like my mediation. Easy-paced running, that is. It allows me to untether myself from the stresses of daily life.

Chapter 12

Bad Idea

Sometimes your best intention is really just a bad idea wrapped up in a bow. My racing mojo was so-so. I was tired of road racing. I was tired of so-so times and so-so training and the races in northern Wisconsin. I hated black flies and humidity. A 10k sounded boring. Jake was hitting the height of toddler-hell so I needed a distraction. I needed something that provided a little mom-time and helped me focus on my health. But it needed to be something new. I did what every sleep-deprived mom does when attempting to fix herself – I turned to Google. I don't recall what I put in the search bar. I'm pretty sure the word "misery" wasn't involved, but it led me down a rabbit hole that helped me realize that sometimes an idea is just straight-up bad.

I decided to do a trail half marathon at Mount Bohemia in the UP of Michigan. I'm a midwestern girl, so my concept of a "mountain" is more akin to a really big hill. Back in my news days, I'd done a story on Mount Bohemia. It is one of those super-ultra-hip hidden ski resorts that focus on black diamond runs, yurt-style warming houses, ramen lunches, no trail grooming and some of the steepest slopes east of the Rockies. In other words, totally badass for this fat ass.

You're probably wondering," what were you thinking?" Or maybe by this point in the book you're like, "Wow she's really a glutton for punishment" (aka an idiot). But seriously, I thought if I did this race it would set a new bar for me. My sentiment was similar to that of race number one: I could do anything I set my mind to. I also love the Upper Peninsula of Michigan. Did I mention the race was during fall peak colors and around the time of my wedding anniversary? It seemed like the perfect family vacation/race day/goal to knock me back onto the wellness track. Also, it was far enough away that I couldn't train on the course, which minimized the likelihood that I would talk myself out of it because the route was too hard.

I started to train. In other words, I bought trail running shoes. This time, I had all the confidence in the world walking into Duluth Running Company and saying, "I use neutral road shoes and need a comparable fit, but for trail running." After much debate and analysis, I ended up abandoning Brooks for a pair of Sauconies. These super-comfortable shoes worked on the trails but were also light enough for the road. I also purchased a knock-off Camelbak and a new trucker-style hat. I have to admit: that first day I felt pretty badass.

I started simple. I figured the best way to train for a trail run was to find a relatively flat trail and run on it. So I did. I always thought the black flies were ruthless on the road. Turns out trail running delves into a new level of black fly-hell. I invested in some high-concentration DEET bug spray. There was nothing all-natural or refreshing about bathing in the stuff from head to toe before heading out. As soon as I started sweating, the chemicals would run into my eyes and mouth. I'm pretty confident that if anyone had lit a match within a hundred yards of me, I would have gone up in a ball of flames. Nevertheless, training was officially underway.

As time progressed, I found my rhythm. I also discovered that while I'm a predictably slow runner, I'm even more tortoise-like as a trail runner. I have a fear of falling. I'm not super graceful. I do best on flat, even surfaces. By nature, trail running isn't flat or on even surfaces. I decided to keep showing up.

Looking back, I have no idea why I kept at it. Sure, I enjoy escaping to the woods. That said, a walk would have achieved the same goal, without the pressure of a half marathon looming on the horizon. By early September it was clear I needed to up my game… literally. I was still training on relatively flat hills, and while I hadn't bothered to look at a topography map of the course, I knew it would involve plenty of steep stretches. It was, after all, taking place at a ski resort. I started hill training. I hated it. I hated every single second of it. The only redeeming moment was when my heart rate would return to normal and I'd be relieved to discover that my previous climb wouldn't actually kill me. It wasn't just the uphill climb, either. Downhill was almost worse. Remember that fear of falling? Yeah. That's particularly acute on rocky downhill trails. But I kept showing up.

Yep. I keep showing up. I keep going and going and going. I fall and skin my knees. I wipe out in what I'd characterize as a mudslide. I experience welts on my back and nearly lose a toenail. As much as I love being in the woods, I hate every moment of training. But I still don't quit. That fact aside, my heart wasn't in it. I was half-assing my trainings, at best, often cranking my music and slowing my aggressive waddle to a leisurely walk. My two-hour training runs would take three hours. My hill climbing would become hill crawling. It was arguably comical. And then I injured myself…

It wasn't a medically diagnosed injury. It was a Google-head-game injury. I was convinced I'd hurt my heel. I started rolling a tennis ball underneath my foot. But the pain progressed. Looking back, I'm pretty sure it was all in my head, but it gave me an excuse.

At this point, you might expect that I quit the race altogether. Nope. That would have made sense. Instead, I used this imaginary injury to ignore the fact that I hadn't been training. I announced on Facebook that I'd be downgrading my race from a half marathon to either a 10k or 5k, depending on how fast my foot healed. In my mind, I believed it. In my heart, I knew the best case scenario was that I'd be doing a 5k. By the week of the race, I was anxious a 5k was even out of reach, but I registered anyway. At this point, I figured why not? Worst case: I'd do a three -mile stroll through the UP of Michigan during fall peak colors. Best case: I'd set a new PR.

Wowza, was I naïve! I arrived race day morning to pick up my packet. As we pulled up to the ski resort, Mount Bohemia suddenly seemed very large. It was certainly much larger than any hills I had trained on in northern Wisconsin. But it wasn't the size of the hill, as much as how steep it was, that concerned me. I realized that incline matters. It was at this moment that I finally took a moment to study the race course map.

Before you call me a moron, let me be more specific. I had calculated the elevation gains and losses for the half early on. I'd even glanced at it when I was downgrading to the 10k. But there's the summary, and then there's the detail. As someone who lives to plan, I think I avoided this detail because I would have talked myself out of the race. The reality is, the 5K literally went straight up with a slight curve and then straight back down. I also knew this race would be small. What I didn't realize was that come start time, it'd be me and the Northern Michigan University running team (not sure if it was cross country or track, but they had matching shirts,) and a few other random racers including a senior with his dog. I had never felt so underprepared in my life.

This is where some motivational music pipes into the narrative, and a fierce-but-supportive imaginary coach yells, "BUT DID YOU FINISH?!" I'm supposed to shout back, "Hell Yeah!". Except no. It didn't play out quite like that. I made a noble attempt to start the run uphill and within a few minutes, I knew I was way out of my league. Everything hurt. My calves, heart, head, knees and most of all, my pride.

I'm not proud of the self-sabotage I served myself over the next forty minutes. My inner dialog was more cruel than that fourth grade fake boyfriend who once asked me, "Why would you even think I really liked you?" Even though he had invited me over to his house and let his dalmatian attack me during a game of hide-and-seek. I digress. The bottom line is I was mean. So incredibly mean to myself. Despite this, I continued to put one foot in the front of the other. It wasn't enough. I hate hills under the best of circumstances. Add in slippery rocks, uneven terrain, and sandy inclines with minimal wayfinding, and I was in my own personal hell. My mind let every ounce of my being know what an idiot I was for thinking I should run this race. I'm sure the few stragglers who heard my conversation with myself thought I was borderline crazy. Frankly, I'm convinced that people who find joy in running straight up a hill, only to turn around and come down, are a bit unhinged, themselves.

I eventually finished. It was hard as hell. And no, this wasn't one of those races where I pushed myself really hard and afterward said "I'm so glad I did it!" Nope. This was one of those lessons in the notion that you get what you give. I went in knowing I hadn't trained hard. I went in knowing that at my size, that's a really bad idea. I'm not a medical professional, but even I knew that what I did was dumb. But I had this vision of who I wanted to be, in my head. Trail runners are super cool. They make it look so easy. I love the clothes. I wanted so bad to be one as long as I didn't have to do the work. So, I didn't do the work. And ignoring that I didn't do the work only made me suffer that much more on trail day. I'm just grateful that the only long-term injury from that day was to my pride.

I paid a decent chunk of change to learn that lesson the hard way. I've never returned to trail running. I still hike and walk and enjoy the grandeur of the wilderness. I thrive in it. But with the comfort of my hiking boots and a tortoise-like waddle.

Know When to Quit

I am uber-stubborn. I despise quitting. I don't readily admit defeat. And yet, I struggle to listen to this piece of advice. I'm constantly reminding myself of it. You can be on a quest for continuous improvement and set crazy goals, and occasionally pivot or abandon a plan. It isn't an either/or commitment. And when you pivot, it doesn't mean you've abandoned your dreams, but rather that the tactic you've been using isn't working. Do I entirely strive to be like Lindsey Vonn? Absolutely. I idolize her strength, determination, commitment and passion. Do I ski? Hell, no.

I can admire trail runners without being one. Mirna Valerio AKA *The Mirnavator* is a huge inspiration in my life, and one of the reasons I hit the trail. If you've ever longed to be a trail runner but struggle with body image, or frankly anything, you must read her book *A Beautiful Work in Progress*. Such a great read. But if I'm being completely honest, the trail is where I go to relax. It's where I go to remember who I am and where I'm going. To rediscover my breath, meditate and practice gratitude.

I learned on Mount Bohemia that I'm not willing to give that up to prove to myself that fat people can trail run. I don't want to associate a gorgeous overlook with cardiac arrest, sprained ankles or skinned-up knees. The thing is, I'm choosing that. I now know that I can finish a trail run. Maybe someday I'll decide the cost is worth the reward. But for now, it just isn't for me. The greatest piece of advice

I can share with you on this subject is that if your gut is telling you that, listen. If you think you're injured, rest. There's no heroism in running yourself literally, or figuratively, into the ground. Sure, push yourself and then go another 10 steps and achieve greatness. But don't be one of the morons who take chances that aren't worth taking, because they think they know better, only to find themselves stuck on a ski hill hating themselves and risking a long-term injury.

Chapter 13

Running Groups

If you're still reading this book, you've probably caught a whiff of my desire to be alone. So this shouldn't come as a huge surprise. I'm the world's biggest introvert. I genuinely don't like people. I love getting to know an individual person one-on-one, hearing about their life and having a meaningful connection. But I despise things like bar-hopping, making small talk with strangers, and networking. The so-called "mixers" marketing folks are supposed to attend are a form of hell for me. This creates quite the conundrum on the running front, since in order to get a piece of running swag, I need to line up with hundreds or thousands of strangers. The small talk is limited, due to my inability to breathe, but there's still the dreaded bus ride one must take to the start line. The one where I sit by myself and am eventually forced to share my seat with a stranger, because of the race organizer's desire to pack us in like sardines to ensure some unwelcome running bonding experience.

The conversations are always pleasant. "Is this your first race?" Words of encouragement. Tips and tricks. Nervous banter. Running jitters. It all comes to life on the bus. Often, I'm surrounded by running groups, though. Mother/daughter pairs. Girlfriends pursuing their goals. Husband/wife teams who use this as a way to connect. FYI: my husband would rather die. And of course there are running groups. Oh, so many running groups. You can pick them out immediately. Not to stereotype…but I'm going to anyway. It's usually a group of twelve to fifteen gals with really large personalities and this unusual bond that results in a ton of laughter, encouragement and an occasional burst of song. There's the matching t-shirts or headbands and team warm-ups at the start. They make running look fun.

I must admit, I'm always a bit jealous of these gals. The downside of being an introvert is that in order to connect on that level, you have to start by joining a casual running group with strangers. You have to put yourself out there and run the risk of being the one who slows the whole group down during a Thursday night run. You're suddenly thrust into a situation where you have to make small talk before the run, and maybe even indulge in a beer and social interaction after your run. That's a lot for an introvert to take in. So I'd always passed on the running clubs. Then one day, eight years into my running journey, I thought, "Why not give it a shot?"

Let's be clear. This was not a *running group*. It was *running with a couple of gals*. It was 2019 and I was training for Grandma's Half Marathon. I had once again lost my mojo (I know I'm sounding like a broken record but I'm being honest, folks) and a woman I graduated high school with was recovering from an injury, and had a solid running team of ladies who seemed nice. They ran on Sunday mornings and I thought that maybe if I just joined them one or two times, it'd push me to train harder. So I did. Guess what? It made all the difference in the world. Now, when Sunday mornings rolled around, I knew there was a gaggle of gals who would be waiting in a parking lot for me. This meant no hitting snooze or rolling over. Sure, I could text and bail, but could I really? I'm a rule follower and I had reached out to her, so it seemed snobby to be a no-show. Nobody would have judged me, really. But my innate desire to follow the rules totally pushed me ahead on that one.

I also discovered that it becomes harder to quit after three miles if the person you are running with is planning six miles and is just far enough ahead of you that you cannot quite yell loudly enough, "Hey! I'm going to bail!" By the time you pause for a bathroom break and to catch up, you're four or five miles in and you might as well finish. So yes, there's that. There's also this thing that isn't as immediately obvious to those of us who are new or still uncertain if they are fit enough to call themself a runner. That is the knowledge that it's hard for everyone. Sure, some folks enjoy it more than others. Some people enjoy a leisure run that makes me green with envy, because a run that slow would have me in cardiac arrest. Sure, some runners are 150% muscle mass and -20% fat. But even they have bad running days. I'm not exactly saying misery loves company, but well, I'm saying misery loves company.

It's that simple. Even if you have no desire to make small talk with strangers, after a ten-mile run on hot pavement, you can have a meaningful five-minute bitch session in which you rediscover that running is hard for everyone. If it were super easy, everyone would do it. Everyone who signed up for a marathon would show up on race day. Everyone who started training on day one would still be training on week fifteen. The reality is that most people don't. And it's during those conversations that you find your tribe. It's in the experience of doing something really difficult together that you find yourself okay with singing silly songs on a bus, comparing war wounds, and enjoying the fitness expo the night before to the point where you maybe even consider participating in the all-you-can-eat spaghetti feed. I'm not there, yet.

But this did change my perspective. This gaggle of gals motivated and inspired me in ways I'm sure they didn't realize. I'm forever grateful. The downside was that I started training with them only about four weeks before Grandma's. I lived thirty-five miles away and only connected with them for the Sunday long runs. But those runs and conversations meant something. When they reached out to me prior to Grandma's to see if I wanted to stay with them the night before, or meet up at 3:30 am to take the cursed bus ride up north together, I politely passed. I wasn't quite ready for that commitment, but I had tiptoed into what can be gained by running with a group.

Race day I ran alone. Or as alone as one can be in a race with over 25,000 participants. I turned up my music, looked straight ahead and counted the moments until I'd see my family at the finish line. That's the thing with running – when you line up, the only motivator you have is yourself and your results are a direct reflection of what you put in, not what a team has accomplished together. That said, it's those folks along the way that make the journey feel worthwhile.

It turns out those four long Sunday runs mattered. Or, maybe it was the fact this was the first urban run I'd completed, so I had the pleasure – and displeasure – of spectators lining the course for most of the 13.1 miles. I kept telling myself that I just needed to get past these folks, and then I'd walk when nobody could see me. Granted, nobody was even looking at me, but that didn't matter. At the end of it all, I had my best race in history. I never walked. I knew that as much as I hurt, everyone around me hurt just as much. In fact, some might even hurt more.

Following that race, a co-worker-turned-good-friend suggested she might want to run a half marathon in October. It was late June. I knew she could do it and I knew I didn't want to run another half. I was tired. Not just physically, but emotionally. I knew how unpleasant training in the summer sun was, how irritating the black flies were, and how humid and sweaty our runs would be. Yet, when she asked, I found the word "sure" escaping my lips.

Once in, I'm all in. Add in an accountability partner that I genuinely love and there was no turning back. Over the next three months we trained together. We laughed together. We sweated together. There was the nine-mile run in which one of us was perhaps a bit dehydrated after indulging the night before, which resulted in Gatorade runs by a significant other. There was packet pick-up together, and come race day, riding the bus together. After eight years of running, I finally had a bus mate. Someone to take selfies with at the start line and share meaningful words of encouragement with. My tribe was complete.

I know at this point you may ask, "Did you meet your running goal?" Running goals are a moving target (no pun intended). I knew my capacity that summer. My only goal was to show up and finish with my friend. My training and eating reflected that. The truth is, I suffered a lot in that race from undertraining. The weather was horrific, resulting in chafing that I can't even begin to describe. I didn't lose a toenail. Granted, there was a point in the course where I literally thought I might die, or that I should hitchhike home. The problem with this course was that it's on an old railroad bed that cuts through about twelve miles of forest so the first time you see real roads, cars and humans is about a mile from the finish. So there's that logistical motivator as well.

No, a running group won't carry you over the finish line. They will motivate you, inspire you, and give you a safe space to share and commiserate in all the miserable aspects of running. They give you snazzy t-shirts and a friend to lean on. They make you laugh and occasionally, maybe, pee your pants a little. They remind you to stay hydrated and tell you to keep going when you want to turn around. In a world where so many women put each other down, this tribe renewed my hope in the power of connection and shared meaning.

Over the years, my running tribe connections were often virtual. My running community is often composed of gals I never run a single day with, but instead share meaningful tips, tricks and stories from the trail. This past year, that changed. I now look forward to time on the trail with friends, invest in the hard work of running, and then finish strong with a breakfast brunch and cocktails, where war wounds and running highs and lows are shared. I never started running for this specific benefit, but I'm forever grateful that these tribes exist. Many of these gals are sharing their stories in this book. As you can tell, I'm a very lucky woman blessed to have so many amazing people in my life.

Tips

I'm still relatively new to running groups, so my tip is simple. Find a group and just show up. You'll know if they are your people. A great place to start is the local shoe store that analyzed your gait. Or throw out a post on social media and watch friends you never even knew were runners crawl out of the woodwork offering to do a Saturday morning run.

I live in a town of 1,100 and a county of 12,000 people. We have no stoplights. But, we have at least four running groups within thirty minutes of my house, who meet on various days, with various gals, at various ability levels. Once you find some groups, ask a few basic questions. What's the commitment level? Cost? Level of fitness? Male, female or co-ed? Then take a chance and show up. Worst case: you bail and find a new group. Best case: you discover your tribe and a new layer of appreciation for the sport of running.

I Have Run
Tara Kay

At 14, I started running. It wasn't really because of a love for cardiovascular exercise. My speedy, sinewy, 110-lb. best friend had been recruited to the cross-country team at our small sub-suburban high school, and I sure didn't want to miss out on any opportunities to socialize. Every fall Saturday, we bussed to golf courses near and far, donned our district-dictated Crayola-green uniforms, and ran a two-mile loop through rolling hills, over tee boxes, and flanking water hazards.

I was a fair-to-middling high school runner, trotting and chatting my way through the twelve-week season alongside another mediocre classmate. Jen was better, but even she could not compete with a senior runner from the reputedly wealthy high school across town. This girl would place first not by seconds, but by minutes.

"Not Kara again," we would all grumble.

(Note: Our rival would grow up to be Olympian Kara Goucher.)

I have run as a size 4. For most of my life, I've been naturally, though not extremely, thin. I've exercised consistently since the aforementioned day I joined the Proctor Cross Country team, and have been equipped with genetics that ensured I could sometimes eat an entire box of Oatmeal Crème Pies without doing any damage. Interestingly, though, my PR half marathon did not come during my two plus, light-on-my-feet decades as a size 4; it came a bit later, at age 36, when work and life pushed me up a digit or two. Go figure.

I have run very, very pregnant (decidedly not a size 4). OK, it was more a waddle, but I did finish a run-walk half marathon while seven-and-a-half months pregnant, wearing a T-shirt which read, "Oops."

I have run without boobs. That section about being a size 4? Yeah, well, there's a negative to that – more specifically, two negatives. I mean, I was basically negative two. Never massive in the 'mamms to begin with, pregnancy, breastfeeding, and an aggressively trained, 12% body fat post-baby body caused my IBTCs to GTFO. Completely. I mean, nothing. I could have used postage stamps instead of a sports bra and my gait would have been completely unaffected. I did post some pretty great times during this, my Top-Light era.

I have run with boobs. In 2014, my chest's topographical resemblance to Kansas (though, did you know Kansas isn't the flattest state in the union? Surprisingly, it's Florida.) began to bother me a great deal, eating away at my already shaky self-esteem. I struggled to find clothes that fit. The thought of intimacy made me want to hide. I felt unattractive, unsexy, and unwomanly. An unconventional workplace conversation inspired me to seek out an alternative to life as a highway. And I got a boob job.

My first run after getting large chemical balls inserted into my chest was almost as scary as that first poop after labor & delivery. Yeah, you know what I'm talking about. Not wanting to ruin something I'd never before had, I waited the full recommended eight weeks before stuffing these heavy round objects into a serious compression bra and setting out the door. It was achy. Uncomfortable. And I was slow. Slow, slow, slow. (I've since adjusted.)

I have run my way through, and finally away from, an abusive relationship. For many years. No bruises. Tantrums. Gaslighting. Broken things. Constant criticism of my body, even at my thinnest; constant criticism of my brain, even as I worked hard to cover all the bills. I packed and unpacked more than a dozen times, and for a stretch that lasted months, I always had a Rubbermaid "go tub" in the back of my Subaru. I would leave for a run to process him losing another job. I would leave for a run, pushing my son in a jogging stroller so he wouldn't have to hear it. I would leave for a run just as the out-of-body screaming would start. I would leave for a run, until finally, I left.

I have run incredibly hung over. A couple of years ago, a group of friends – a couple from the Proctor Cross Country team, even – got together to run a relay on the famed (and really hilly) American Birkebeiner course. I'd had a tough week at work and slugged far too much of our hostess's white wine. After insisting everyone recite the words to American Pie – one of my favorite tests of musical acumen - I fell asleep in a lower "grandkid" bunk, cute, olive green office dress still on.

I woke up fuzzy, dry, headachy, the whole bit. I staggered around the room collecting my running gear lumbered into the pickup truck which would be shuttling us to the various checkpoints along the trail. I rested my head against the cool window, praying for death and deeply regretting that I had volunteered to replace a last-minute dropout and run not just one, but two legs of the notoriously difficult race. I did it. But did it ever suck.

I have run with my face poking through a giant Mona Lisa frame. Yup, that was a Halloween race. It was a little awkward with the wind. I even won a big bucket of candy!

I have run perfectly trained, fed and hydrated (though not that often). There have been a couple of periods in my 42 years where I took running seriously. I printed out training plans and hung them all over my home and office. I would scout a route in advance, precisely track the miles on my OG Garmin, and stage water bottles every couple of miles. I read the books and magazines and planned the meals and did all the stretches and got all the sleep. And you know what? It would pay off. My best performances and best recoveries came along when I put in the work. But putting in the work doesn't always fit in every season of life, so we do the best we can. As runners, we can always be proud.

I have run just to run. And I'll keep running as long as I'm able. As the me I am now, or as whichever me shows up next.

Chapter 14

The Bus

In 2019, I was over running. I'm not talking about a minor, intermittent desire to not train. Instead, this was a full-fledged "fuck you!" to running. I was tired of being the fat girl in the back, but not motivated enough to actually do something about it. I was tired of sore joints, flopping boobs, and sweat-stained baseball caps. I was tired of lining up in a sea of lycra knowing that 99% of the folks lining up beside me will destroy me on the course. But there's another problem. My father-in-law loves that I run. He loves asking me how my running is going. He loves giving me tips and getting recaps of my experiences. I've never once mentioned my times or where I finish in these races, just that I finished. I love hearing his running stories and talking running tips. It was a connection I cherished and one of the many reasons I couldn't quite walk (or run) away from the sport I hated. But, I'll be frank, after eight years and more than twenty races I was ready to retire. I was ready to quit. Right until I didn't.

It started with the scale tipping a number I hadn't seen since pregnancy. In my defense, the spike occurred during a three-month period when I changed jobs, wrote a thesis and completed my MBA, and my father underwent an amputation that resulted in a 60+ day hospital stay and multiple near-death encounters. Throw in Christmas and a kindergartener who was demonstrating high levels of irrational independence, and I was physically, mentally and emotionally depleted. My emotional eating was at an all-time high and I thoroughly enjoyed a lot of Christmas cookies and holiday parties that winter. But I'm not an idiot. Even I have my limits, and I knew I needed to do something.

So I did what every procrastinator does when contemplating a weight loss endeavor. I went on Facebook. There I scrolled aimlessly while watching Real Housewives on Bravo. Suddenly, my scrolling stopped at a post by Members Cooperative Credit Union. My friend runs their marketing division and I always enjoy seeing what she's up to in marketing, so it isn't unusual that my memory-muscles generally want me to pause on her posts. But, this one was about running. What's the connection? Turns out they were a title sponsor of Grandma's Marathon in Duluth. And with just a simple post, featuring my favorite running quote, I can win a guaranteed entry. For those who don't know, the Garry Bjorklund Half Marathon is lottery-based, and by now the race was full. On a whim, I thought, "Why not?" This single action was sufficient to make me feel like I was doing something about my current state, and I figured if I won, I'd be motivated enough to show up. Plus, I never win anything, so I figured I was pretty safe.

You can guess what happened next. I won. And because I hadn't really read the post, I thought I had won a free guaranteed entry to the race. I had until May 1 to claim it and it was mid-January. It turned out "guaranteed" and "free guaranteed" entries are two different things and I actually had to pay the $100 entry fee, but it'd be months before I figured that factoid out. I had twenty-one weeks until race day. From the comfort of my couch, I had a similar epiphany to my hungover self of eight years ago, and I figured, "Why not? What have I got to lose?" I immediately jumped into planning mode. I bought a new pair of shoes. I invested in Lauren Fleshman and Roisin McGettigan-Dumas's training journal. I updated my playlist. Thanks to the power of Pinterest, I created motivational quote boards and some stretching suggestions. I did everything but run.

Then one day, I visited the race website. It was there, while scrolling through the details, that I stumbled across the bus. The bus. Those words would haunt me for the next twenty-one weeks. It turned out that there was a maximum finish time of 3:04 – or for those more mathematically challenged – you must run a minimum of a fourteen-minute mile. On the race entry form, you sign off that you can beat that time or a bus may sweep you from the course to ensure room for the full marathon runners. My best half marathon time at the time was 3:16. For those who don't run, twelve minutes may seem like nothing. Those who do run know that those who think that's possible are delusional. At a minimum, you need to be seriously committed to making some long-term lifestyle changes and plan to train hard to make a time like that. My eight years of running demonstrated that I did not fit that category.

Once again, I ignored logic. I posted on Facebook about my next training adventure, knowing that once I put it out there, I'd have to try. I eventually started running. Remarkably, I occasionally hit a fourteen-minute mile. Granted, it was on a treadmill and involved some stops, but it was still a fourteen-minute mile. I started to believe that maybe I could pull this off. I wouldn't say I rediscovered a love for running, but I'd say I was showing up for my training runs and running hard.

Then, life happened. The snow melted and I upgraded my training watch to one with a built-in GPS. The combination of a more accurate read and running outside, versus on my treadmill, (which apparently wasn't calibrated correctly) was eye-opening. It was eye-opening in the sense that I found that my thirteen-minute miles were actually sixteen-minute miles. And, the harder I trained, the slower I seemed to go.

Self-doubt came knocking loudly on my door. Who was I to think I could run this race? Why would I want to run this race? Unlike my other solo adventures in the woods in places where nobody knew me, this was a large national race that was lined with folks watching. How humiliating it would be to finish last in a sea of 10,000 runners. Or, worse yet, to not even finish and instead get swept up by a bus because I was that lame. I may suck at running, but at least I've always finished. I wasn't ready to hit a new low by being removed from a course.

The ominous bus would continue to haunt me for weeks. The former journalist in me started sleuthing about said bus. It wasn't hard to do – I had direct lines with dozens of former finishers and was even friends with someone who used to work on the marathon staff. The more I talked to folks, the more I discovered that perhaps this sweeper bus was an urban legend. A quick look at the previous year's results supported this, with some folks finishing the half marathon in six hours. It created just enough doubt in me to convince me to keep training, despite my constant fear that I'd never get to finish. This continued until April.

April marked my first 5k of the season. It was a beautiful day to catch a glimpse of where I was at in my training. I was running with some new friends. There was a promise of cocktails post-race. It was an uneventful start. I even managed to beat the maybe-mythical bus time by forty-five seconds. But something happened on that course. My legs went completely numb. Literally numb. Not one, or a portion of one, but both of them from the knees down. The last kilometer of the race, I watched my feet pounding the pavement, wondering how they were even moving. It was creepy and another potential excuse to quit.

I immediately scheduled an appointment with my doctor. After much debate and a few tests, we chalked it up to a random and undiagnosable occurrence, but we'd keep monitoring it. I never experienced that feeling sensation again, but for whatever reason, I could no longer run. Each time I went out, my legs throbbed. My ankles hurt. I'd go a few miles and felt utterly exhausted. The clock kept ticking. I watched my training plan get more and more condensed. I fought with my inner self for a month. Was the combination of undiagnosed numbness and injury enough reason to quit? Was the mythical loser-bus going to knock me out of the running? All signs indicated that based on my training schedule and current runs, my anticipated finish time would be 3:15. And I had discovered I would have to pay the $100 entry fee.

My husband and I debated this conundrum endlessly. In his mind, $100 was not a reason to not do it. He even offered to pay the fee. In his mind, he knew no bus driver could ever sweep me off a course or prevent me from getting my medal. He knew I would finish. He trusted and respected my doctor enough to believe that if she said I was cleared to run, then the best cure for me would be to run. He believed I had nothing to lose and nobody but me would care where I finished in the race. I hated his logic.

I turned to Facebook and sought counsel (and excuses) from friends. There were a few folks who advised me to do whatever was best for me. If it was that miserable, then I could quit. They argued that life is too short to force yourself to do something you don't want or need to do. Unfortunately, these comments were scarce. The same inspiration that had convinced me to run eight years ago came flooding forward again. It's easy to support someone else's ambitions from the comfort of your computer screen. It's easy to say, "You can do it." By April 30th, I needed to make a decision. I paid the entry fee. I was in.

I'd like to say that once I committed, it was easy. It wasn't. I was still injured. I was weeks behind on training. I honestly didn't know if I'd even get far enough in my training to have the capacity to run thirteen miles. I kept revising and condensing my already-condensed training time. My 10k in May was downgraded to a 5k and then became my first no-show ever. Things looked grim. The clock kept ticking. My chances of finishing grew dim. And then, after six weeks of dismal training, I turned a corner. My legs no longer throbbed on mile-long jaunts. I looked at the calendar, and with some creative math, I discovered that I could pull off enough long runs to at least finish. But that damn bus kept looming in the back of my mind. I hated that bus. It represented every running insecurity I had ever experienced.

I snapped. Literally. I was on a run listening to Fort Minor's *Remember the Name*. And, I got mad. In that moment, I loved running. I loved the fact that I was running. I loved the fact that I kept showing up, even though it would have been so much easier to quit. It was in this moment that I decided that I was tired of questioning whether I was good enough to run. I was running—but on my terms. Fuck the bus!

From that moment on, I showed up for my runs. I quit caring about my time and focused on finishing the miles. For the first time ever, I ran with a couple of incredible ladies. What started as a five-mile run ended with 9.6 miles and it was fun! I kept going. There was no time for tapering. And then it was race week. I carbo-loaded with conviction. I dragged my husband to the health fair and stocked up on free samples. I posted pictures on Facebook and shared my self-doubts and conviction to finish.

There's a lot of talk about how challenges are more about the journey than the destination. By race day morning I knew I'd finish. I knew I had it in me to show up and give it my best. I also had peace with the knowledge that thousands of runners would beat me. My goal was to finish strong. To pace myself and cross the finish line with my head held high. After mile one, I threw that goal out the window. I decided to just run. To quit caring about time or pacing or ensuring I had enough reserves to get across the finish. I decided to be foolish and break all the rules and just run. And, so I did.

I ran for the love of running. I thought of my mom and how proud she'd be of me for not quitting. She never cared about what I wanted to be when I grew up, only that I'd try hard and make my own path. I ran for my dad, who could no longer run, but wanted nothing more than to go for a long walk. I ran for my son, to show him that it isn't about winning, but showing up and trying. I ran for my friends, who said my journey inspired them and convinced them to try something out of their comfort zone. I ran for every fat girl who sits on the sidelines and thinks they aren't built to run. But most importantly, I ran for me. After eight years of showing up at starting lines, I realized that as much as I hate the process of running, I love the act of running. I love that every morning that I wake up, I get to decide if I want to run. I can blow off the training and eat the chips or I can train hard. I get to choose how much or how little I want to do, and then see those results embodied on the road. I get to experience the camaraderie of running, buy overpriced shoes, listen to hip hop and channel my inner grit.

At the end of the day, I'm a stubborn Finlander. At times, there's a thin line between stubborn and stupid. But that day, my Sisu was strong. I knew when I finally crossed the finish line it would be my best time ever. But more importantly, I had run the race on my terms, finally at peace with the person I am, on and off the course. For anyone wondering, I didn't beat the cut-off time. I missed it by four minutes. But the ominous bus? It never showed up. It turned out that I was good enough just as I was.

The Bus

I recognize that cut-off times are a real thing. They should be respected, and in many cases those cut-off times will be enforced. I strongly encourage every runner to read all of the race details before dropping an entry fee, especially if a finisher's medal or post-race swag is a major motivator for you. And, frankly you should do so out of respect for the dozens or hundreds of volunteers it takes to pull off an event. That said, there are races that respect the back of the pack and there are those that do not.

I've been in a race where they ran out of shirts and those running the shorter distance were SOL. I've crossed a finish line only to learn the finisher food had already been packed up. I've made it to a water station where they've run out of water, and in one case, weren't even manning it anymore. In all of these instances, I'd showed up at the designated start time and was well within the racing window. These are races I'd probably not line up at again. But for every one of those, there are many exceptions.

I've appreciated the crossing guards who halted traffic at major intersections in advance, to ensure I wouldn't have to slow down. Frankly, if I stopped it would be all over, but my PR matters, too. There have been the volunteers who gave me high-fives, rang cowbells, shouted words of encouragement, and even offered heavily spirited shots. Fellow runners are also a constant source of encouragement. My favorites are the finishers who use the course for their cool-down. At first, I found this highly irritating. But it's on the courses where this is allowed that I've discovered that race officials have found a balance between embracing the competition while keeping the spirit of running alive.

You Ran a Few Races, Big Deal

This is the thought running through my head as I make the crucial decision of whether to ask some of my running friends who've inspired me over the years to contribute to my book. I know if I ask them, they'll say yes. I'm fortunate to have fabulous friends and role models who love to empower people.

Knowing this, I struggle with whether to ask them or not, because if I do, it'd mean no turning back. There would be nothing standing in the way of self-publishing my first book. My ego didn't like that. Who on this planet gives a rat's ass that my fat ass crossed a finish line? Absolutely nobody... but me.

So why not? It's the same logic I used for running and that turned out okay. As a glutton for punishment, I would naturally choose the year a pandemic hit to attempt penning a book. I obviously didn't know going into 2020 what a shit-show circus it'd be. But I started this year off with a crazy adventure, and I made a commitment to myself.

I attended my first-ever personal development conference. I wanted to take 2020 to reset – to remind myself of what really matters, and to make some necessary changes in my life to be more authentic. By all accounts, it was a weekend of wow. I learned so much about my inner workings and the unnecessary pressure I put on myself to be my version of perfection. I left the weekend with the 2020 power word of Grace.

I also set my intention of self-publishing a book. This book. It had been brewing in my heart for nearly a decade. I had over a dozen starts and stops. My main, and only, motivator for writing it is that I wish this narrative existed when I was trying to determine if I was good enough to take those first steps on the race course.

Then COVID-19 hit. Can we just acknowledge this situation with an appropriate "WTF?!" Every race on my to-do list this year was cancelled. Other than a few lackluster road jaunts, my running is null right now. This is partially due to being in survival mode, and partly to rediscovering my passion for taking long walks while streaming podcasts. I don't experience the same joy for running, without a tangible race or focal point in front of me. That's my motivator, folks. Virtual runs just don't cut it, so I find myself feeling a bit like a fraud hitting publish on a book about running when I'm not even running. The thing about giving yourself grace, though, means publishing anyway.

Here's the thing. I know without a doubt I'll return to running. It'll be on my terms, at my pace, at my size. I'll line up with the cool kids in the back and chat about the difficult challenges we're about to overcome. I'll linger in the running stores awaiting an industry that will finally acknowledge that their template for an athletic clothing customer is not reflective of those who actually show up on race day. That grit and determination and a desire to belong doesn't discriminate.

If you've read this far, it means there is a calling in your heart to run. Please do. Love it. Hate it. Ultimately make a decision if you want to run a race. But if you take nothing else from this book, don't let others make that decision for you. You have the power and strength to run a race. You don't need to change a thing or be anyone but who you are in this moment. Will it be hard as fuck? Yes. Will it hurt? Yes. Will you want to quit? Yes. Will it change you? Maybe. At least you'll be the author of your own narrative. You'll be writing your history with every step you take. No matter what anyone says, that matters. If I can tell you just one last thing, it's that if I can run, you can run. So, if that's what you want to do, then go run, my friend, and whatever you do, cherish your toenails and carry some toilet paper.

Acknowledgements

This book was written by me thanks to the encouragement and assistance of many people. A special thanks to the brave ladies who shared their stories and inspiration. I hope wisdom packed advice from Meredith Ziegler, Carrie Okey, Carrie Alajoki, Alisa Kolwitz, Tami Unseth, Roberta King, Tara Kay, and Courtney Montoya motivate and encourage you to head out on the open road. Without them, I never would have had the courage to lace up and to keep lacing up with things got difficult. To my former office mate and incredible designer Kate Deering, thank you for your patience while we negotiated whether my ass should grace the cover (I won that right). A special thanks to Lara Wilkinson for believing in this project enough to take time out of her extremely busy schedule editing my words into coherent sentences and thoughts. Without this tribe of women and many, many others this book would have remained a *what if...*

To the men and women who have volunteered for hours so that I can experience the runner's high of crossing that finish line, I thank you. To my husband Steve for supporting my running and writing and all the drama that comes with both, I want you to know I love and appreciate you. And to my 7-year old son who keeps me grounded and humble every single day, I hope someday you read this book and know that your mama is many things, but she is not a quitter.

My heart is full. Thank you.

This is in no way a comprehensive list of running resources, just a few of the game-changing tools that have helped me cross the finish line.

Books and Training Journals:

Brown, B. (2012). *Daring greatly.*

Dais, D. (2006). *The non runner's marathon guide for women. Get off your butt and on with your training.*

Duckworth, A. (2016). *Grit. The power of passion and perseverance.*

Flanagan, S. & Kopecky, E. (2018). *Run Fast. Cook Fast. Eat Slow. Quick-fix recipes for hangry athletes.*

Fleshman, L. & McGettigan, R. (2016). *Compete training journal.*

Goucher, K. (2018). *Strong.*

Graham, J. (2012). *Honey, do you need a ride? Confessions of a fat runner.*

Heminsley, A. (2013). *Running like a girl.*

McDowell, D. & Shea, S. (2009). *Run like a mother. How to get moving – and not lose your family, job, or sanity.*

Valerio, M. (2017). *A beautiful work in progress.*

Van Der Kolk, V. (2015). *The body keeps the score: Brain, mind and body in the healing of trauma.*

Digital Resources to follow:

Runs for Cookies: runsforcookies.com

Badass Lady Gang: badassladygang.com

Runner's World: runnersworld.com